Memories of

Stroud

Memories of

Stroud

TAMSIN TREVERTON JONES

TEMPUS

In memory of my father
Terry Thomas
1932-1998

Frontispiece: Painting of Stroud High Street by Terry Thomas. This painting was given to Anne Mackintosh as a gift from Terry during the High Street campaign in 1980.

First published 2005

Tempus Publishing Limited
The Mill, Brimscombe Port,
Stroud, Gloucestershire, GL5 2QG

© Tamsin Treverton Jones, 2005

The right of Tamsin Treverton Jones to be identified as the Author
of this work has been asserted by him in accordance with the
Copyrights, Designs and Patents Act 1988.

All rights reserved. No part of this book may be reprinted
or reproduced or utilised in any form or by any electronic,
mechanical or other means, now known or hereafter invented,
including photocopying and recording, or in any information
storage or retrieval system, without the permission in writing
from the Publishers.

British Library Cataloguing in Publication Data.
A catalogue record for this book is available from the British Library.

ISBN 0 7524 3437 3

Typesetting and origination by Tempus Publishing Limited
Printed in Great Britain

Contents

Introduction

Stroud has a puzzling sense of identity. It is a town that has attracted, and continues to attract, people who love its bohemian atmosphere, its promise of healthy living, its thriving Farmer's Market, organic cafés and natural therapists. Check the notice board at Withey's Yard and you will find poetry readings and storytelling, meditation, yoga classes and clog dancing. The artistic community is vibrant and the Open Studios Festival a yearly treat.

But this is only half the story: dig down another layer to find the bedrock of Stroud people, born and raised at the top of town, who played at Snakeshole or Daisy Bank, who shopped at the Cross, who were apprenticed at Daniels or Redler's or who worked at Sperry's or Hoffmann's during the war. These people lived through Stroud's heyday, when the churches were packed on Sundays and when it was a town so stuffed with shops that it was hard to know which fishmonger's or butcher's to choose, which cake shop, hardware store or draper's (there was, of course, only one place to buy your sweets, though). 'Your world literally ended at Rodborough Common,' says Dennis Mason, 'People laugh at me now when I say that, but you had no reason to go anywhere else; we had everything here: the Golden Valley.' And it was.

But nothing stands still and a few years later than most places, this old hill town found itself being redesigned, in an attempt to bring it up to date. This led to a series of important protests: in the face of unacceptable change to their environment, the people of Stroud, in the words of Julian Usborne, 'found their voice'. 'This is what Stroud is all about,' says Jane Wells, a founder of Stroud's hugely successful charity, the Meningitis Trust, 'If we think we can do something, we get on and do it!'

Stroud's historical links with the cloth industry were enthusiastically described to me by Jack Marshall and it was a pleasure to discover that Daniels, one of the town's biggest employers for many years, were not only honest and caring, but also eccentric innovators, unswervingly loyal to family and staff. Fiercely loyal too are Howard Beard, David Russell and Jim Fern, whose stories reflect years of thought and research into the town and area they love.

You might still be struck by the ugly car park or the unfathomable road system and you can't compare this town to its smarter but more predictable neighbour, Cirencester, but there is an unpretentious quality to Stroud, a complex and unusual mixture of the old and the new, and this is where the answer to the puzzle seems to lie. It's in the buildings, ancient and modern, and it's in the people too: whether they are Stroud 'born and bred' or 'blow ins' as described, unforgettably, by Maggie Mills, the range of contributors to this book reflects the unique character of the town.

Tamsin Treverton Jones

Acknowledgements

I would like to thank all my contributors for their time, their stories and their photographs, all freely given.

I would also like to thank a few people in particular, without whom this book would not have been possible: Howard Beard, who has been exceptionally generous with his photographic collection, and David Russell, who has helped enormously with research. Many thanks to Jim Fern for allowing use of his article, 'The Birth, Life and Death of a Renowned Stroud Engineering Company known as Daniels', and thanks to Peta Bunbury, a good friend who takes a great portrait. Thanks to Joyce Gray, Michael Mills and Lionel Walrond, and to Anne Mackintosh for her advice and for the loan of my father's painting. To Councillor John Marjoram for his contribution and to Matilda Pearce at Tempus. Finally, thanks to my husband, Greg, who is always so supportive and a great source of inspiration.

Demonstrators during the High Street campaign, 1980.

List of Contributors

Eric Armstrong, Howard Beard, Ron Birch, Jonathan Daniels, Juliana Daniels, May Bell Dullea, Jim Fern, Alan Ford, Peggy Fowler, Geoff Franklin, Mike Goodenough, Dora Grange, Ron Grange, Michael Gray, Reg Hancock, Dorothy Harding, Irene Hopwood, Edie Lee, Anne Mackintosh, John Marjoram, Jack Marshall, Maggie Mills, Michael Mills, Dennis Mason MBE, David Russell, Ena Smith, John V. Smith, Pamela Spokes, Steve Tomlin, Ken Toomer, Julian Usborne, Jane Wells MBE.

one

The Old
Town

The Cross, *c.* 1910. The fountain in the centre of this picture was damaged beyond repair and no longer exists in its original form, but one of the dolphins can still seen at the Museum in the Park in Stroud. (Photograph courtesy of Howard Beard)

The Cross

The 'Berlin Wall' is what prevents you driving straight down the High Street from Nelson Street. It went up about thirty-odd years ago to take the traffic out of the centre of Stroud and on to the mini bypass. The Cross was in front of the old Co-op building at the bottom of Nelson Street and that used to be the market on Saturday nights. It was an open-air market, with light provided by hurricane lamp. That's where all the butchers would bring the meat they had left and if you wanted a bargain you went to the Cross on a Saturday night. It drew the people; it was like a magnet. Not far away was Granny Ball's sweet shop; she was famed for her home-made sweets and when she was making them, you could smell them from twenty yards away.

Dennis Mason, born 1925

Heaving with people

Where the police station is now was just a yard; on the left was the Corn Exchange public house and opposite was the Crown, which had a dance hall above it. The King's Arms was there too. The old light used to swing there on the Cross; that was the centre of Stroud that was. The late-night meat market was there and the whole place was heaving with people! But it was rough around the Cross; Webb's had a big coal yard on the right and further up on

The Cross in 1959, showing the Central Stores for the Stroud Co-operative Society, built in 1931. Tower Hill rises to the left and Nelson Street to the right of the Co-op building. The houses on Tower Hill were demolished and the site is now a car park. (Photograph courtesy of Peckham's of Stroud)

the left was George Osborne's scrap metal where you used to take rabbit skins; he'd have them off you for a few ha'pennies.

Reg Hancock, born 1925

There was quite an atmosphere

There were no fridges or freezers then, and the shops, which had perishable food, would sell it off cheap at the end of the week. A lot of people went shopping at the Cross on a Saturday night and get a joint of meat for about threepence or a threepennyworth of stewing steak. It's hardly believable the prices, I can't believe them myself sometimes. There was quite an atmosphere. The stalls would be all along the Shambles by the parish church. There used to be a chappie with china and glass and he used to auction it; loads of people came. Granny Ball lived up Hill Street where she had her sweet shop and she took a stall down there. Loads of people went to Granny Ball for their sweets. She used to do black and white mints, pink and white mints, acid drops, things like that. You could get a ha'penny worth of sweets in the three-cornered bags and if there was one too many, she never took it out, she used to give it to you. She was good like that. They were beautiful sweets, all made herself. She had them in the big jars and you could pick a mixture of what you wanted.

Dorothy Harding, born 1922

Stroud High Street in the late 1920s. Revell & Sons, boot makers, is on the left. (Photograph courtesy of Howard Beard)

Granny Ball's home-made sweets

We went to Stroud on Saturday evenings: we used to walk up to the Cross, at the top of the High Street. Granny Ball used to have her own home-made sweets and on Saturday she would bring out a stall and I always had a half a pound of cloves; that was my favourite. Her sweets were wonderful. Granny Ball was a dear old soul; she just loved everybody coming in. Stroud was busy on Saturday nights. Father would go there with a list and walk from Ebley and back again.

May Bell Dullea (*née* Curtis), born 1925

Stroud's shops

Shops in Stroud, oh my goodness: there was Lipton's, Mason's, International, Maypole, Strange's and Melias'. Wet Moody's and Fishy Lee's fish shops. Pritchard, Bambridge, Eastman's butchers. Smith and Lee, and Timothy White's hardware shops. Tuck's, Fowler's, Shore's and Walter's cake shops. Bradshaw's, Ball's and Player's fruit shops. There were two cinemas, the Gaumont and the Ritz. There were clothiers, shoe shops, furniture shops, hairdressers, opticians, dentists, bookmakers, dance halls and the like!

Reg Hancock, born 1925

Granny Ball

Granny Ball was like a witch! She had glasses and long grey hair and wore a big coat. I always remember, you went into the shop and the wooden floor sort of sloped down so you would be almost running up to the counter. But the smells! I can smell them now.

Geoff Franklin, born 1946

They X-rayed your feet

In the lower part of the High Street was Revell & Sons, boot makers. It was an old-fashioned shoe shop and it was there until relatively recently. In it was a gadget that X-rayed your feet. With hindsight, I would imagine this was a fairly dangerous process! I can remember having my feet X-rayed many, many times.

Russell Street in the late 1920s. (Photograph courtesy of Howard Beard)

You put them into the bottom of an upright machine and you could look down through the top. Your feet appeared green and you could see how they were fitting into the shoes. I hate to think of the cumulative damage of doing this regularly. There was a gentleman called Mr Burrows, who was the manager of the shop. He must have spent a good deal of his life looking through this X-ray machine with no protection whatsoever.

I also remember Boots in Russell Street. When I was a child, Boots had a sit-on weighing machine, which we all very much enjoyed using. You got on to a seat and some weights were put on next to you and you could be weighed. The person who operated this machine was the redoubtable Eileen Halliday, who has since become famous as the lady who refused to let Sainsbury's take her home away. She was as much a character in those days as she is today.

Bell's the drapers were in the High Street, a bit further up from Revell's, almost at the junction with Kendrick Street. They had this amazing machine for taking your money and giving your change back. The cash was taken by an assistant and placed in a cylinder fixed to a wire high up above the counter. On the pulling of a lever, the cylinder shot off along the wire and disappeared into the cashier's office, which was at the furthest end of the shop. The cashier opened the cylinder, took out the money and the chitty and placed the change back in the cylinder, which then shot back along the wire. It was a very interesting machine.

Howard Beard, born 1943

Everybody delivered

Stroud was starting to go downhill when we left in 1960; things were starting to be ripped down. I remember shops like Lipton's and Home and Colonial and Revell's, the shoe shop down the High Street where you used to get your feet X-rayed. Down Nelson Street was a fruit and vegetable shop: all the fruit used to be out on the road, leaning up against the wall. We used to go to a family butcher's on the edge of Swan Lane called Seabrook and Hughes which had sawdust on the floor.

We didn't have a fridge or a freezer, we didn't have a telly, and we didn't have a car, washing machine, dishwasher or a telephone. We went shopping most days: we had a big larder (with a mouse) and a mesh meat safe, and everybody delivered: the baker used to come every afternoon, the laundry used to come, you'd send the sheets out and they would come back in a long brown paper package. The butcher delivered too. Milk came from Stroud Creamery. There used to be a man who delivered milk called Mr Bolton: he was a small, stringy, unpleasant man, but I used to plead with mother to get her milk from him, because he had a cart and a horse called Dolly. I thought it was an immense carthorse, but she was probably just a cob, she had a docked tail. I knew every inch of Dolly. I was passionate about horses. Lemonade was delivered too: a Corona lorry used to come up every week. Winstone's Ice Cream came up with a bell ringing, too.

Pam Spokes, born 1949

The Co-op in Chapel Street

The Bisley Road was just a dirt track then. The milkman's name was Mr Neal, and Mr Sessions who lived up in Belmont Road used to deliver the bread and the groceries for the Co-op, when you put your order in. The Co-op was in Chapel Street and it was the head offices in those days. They had a butcher's and a grocery shop and what they called the 'Penny Bank' opposite their stables, where you could save money. There was a little Co-op in Horns Road, but nearly everywhere had little Co-ops in those days and nearly every street in Stroud had a pub.

Dorothy Harding, born 1922

A busy place with lots of shops

I served an apprenticeship in Clark's drapery shop in Stroud, where the video shop is now. Stroud was a busy place with lots of shops. On Hill Street, at the Cross, was Granny Ball's home-made sweets, a fish and chip shop; then further down there was a model shop and on the other side was Bell's drapery shop and Smith's chemist, then along the Shambles there was a market on Fridays and Saturdays. There was also Lewis and Godfrey, Woolworth's and Burton's.

I did a year apprenticeship and after I did my exams and had a haberdashery counter of my own. In the shop there was lace and linen and ribbons of every shape and size, then there were stockings, pure silk stockings, a shilling and a penny a pair, as well as the lisle stockings. My counter sold buttons, hooks and eyes, cottons of all descriptions, and wool. Downstairs was the 'Manchester Department', so-called because most of the stuff came from Manchester. I remember that one year we had a flood and it went into the basement and marked all the sheets and pillowcases, so we had to have a sale to get rid of all the stained stuff. People were queuing outside, there were even fights between the women, so we had to close the shop and the manager had to speak sternly to the customers!

May Bell Dullea, born 1925

We used to peep over the stable door

Where Iceland is now was Niblett's, the mineral water establishment. Carry on up Back Lane and there was a slaughterhouse where we used to peep over the stable door and watch animals being killed and bled: sheep and pigs and all. Knight's the coppersmith was opposite and on the corner, where Back Lane entered High Street, was Pritchard's the butcher. On the other corner was what you would today call a delicatessen. That's all gone.

Reg Hancock, born 1925

May Bell Dullea (*née* Curtis) in the 1930s.

Niblett's

Down Swan Lane was Niblett's pop factory. Our neighbour, Mrs Marshall, worked there, so on our way home from school we used to go in and she'd always give us bottles of pop. That was something! Harry Knight, the sheet metal worker, had a workshop up Swan Lane; it had a cobwebby window and you couldn't resist looking in.

Geoff Franklin, born 1946

Moses Smith & Son

My great-grandfather, Moses Smith, started his own company, Moses Smith & Son, in Kings Stanley, which my grandfather Charles continued after his father's death in 1895. In 1906 Smith, Rogers and Co. Ltd, the bacon-curing company at Ebley, was formed. Charles eventually took over two 300-acre farms: Bown Hill above Woodchester and Park Farm in the Severn Valley at Cambridge. He

POMPADOUR'S

E. P. POTTS & A. M. MILLS

KING STREET,   STROUD, Glos.

ARTISTIC HAIRDRESSERS,
BEAUTY CULTURE and CHIROPODY.
Phone 334.

Above and Opposite: The letterheads from three of Stroud's businesses.

grew his own barley and reared a commercial herd of Wessex Saddleback pigs. He bought the corn merchant business W. Knight and Co. at Ebley Oil Mill, and they had a quarter of a mile of pigsties at Eastington. With his own string of retail shops and a contract to distribute throughout Wales, he was doing very well, but sadly it all failed at the beginning of the Great War, as demand had outstripped production. Buying in pigs brought with it swine fever one year and erysipelas the next; disease two years running stopped the bold enterprise. The business was eventually sold to Mattheson's and then to Wall's and Smith's Superfeed Ltd, as it had become. Ebley Corn Mill ceased production in 1994.

John V. Smith, born 1926

Mother's shop
My mother ran an off-licence and faggot shop after the war: faggots and peas on a Tuesday, chicken on a Thursday and pigs' feet on a Friday; I think they were tuppence. People came from all over the place to my mother's shop. They were good faggots; all the meat used to come from Smith Rogers' shop.

Reg Hancock, born 1925

Faggots and peas
Tuesday night was choir practice night and mother would give me an enamel jug which I would take in to a shop halfway down Bisley Old Road – an off-licence and little stores run by Mrs Hancock. She was renowned for her home-made faggots and peas; they were beautiful! I would leave the jug there and go to choir practice, and then, on the way home, I would call in and they were put in there, covered in newspaper – nobody worried in those days about getting your hands dirty – and that was our supper on a Tuesday night, and it was something we always looked forward to. That carried on for a while; it was a must!

Dennis Mason, born 1925

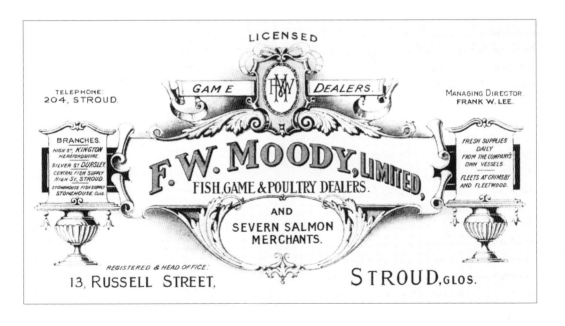

Strange's grocery shop in King Street, *c.* 1903. (Photograph courtesy of Howard Beard)

Strange's was an old-fashioned shop

Strange's was a grocers in King Street. Back in the early 1960s when I was a student I had a job driving for them. I had to take a large blue van with a dozen small boxes of groceries and drive them to places like Slad. It could not have been economical to deliver groceries in that way, but Strange's was an old-fashioned shop and Mr Strange believed that you should offer this service to your customers. I also remember, in about 1963, seeing him go to look – I thought fairly nervously – in the window of the new Co-op store opposite Woolworth's. That was the first supermarket to come to Stroud and you could see that he realised this competition was something that he was not going to be able to match.

After the war, when the first consignment of bananas was able to get through from Jamaica, they arrived in King Street for Mr Strange to put into his cellar to ripen. They were lowered through thick glass doors in the pavement. Anyway, when they were ripe, because my aunt was working next door at the café and knew Mr Strange, I was able to have one of the very first bananas to be had in Stroud after the Second World War.

Howard Beard, born 1943

Coal wagon belonging to T. Butt & Son, 1911. The wagon was built by Gloucester Railway Carriage and Wagon Company Ltd and was one of nine wagons; seven owned by the company and two hired.

From bargees to builder's merchants

My father's name was Hill but my mother's name was Butt and it was my mother's family, my great-grandfather, who started the business, T. Butt & Son in Stroud in 1867. Before that, the Butts were a bargee family who brought coal along the Thames and Severn canal. The last load of coal that we had was in 1926, during the General Strike; after that we brought it in by rail on the Midland Railways. We had seven of our own railway wagons, but they were taken away from us during the war and we never got them back again.

We used to run our own barges but eventually father said we couldn't carry on. The bargees were characters who would sit on the canal bridge and natter away and we would give them toll money, but by the time they got through to Gloucester they would have spent it all in the pubs: the canals were very well served for pubs.

My family lived in Horns Road in the late 1920s and although we were coal merchants in the town, we also had a separate little business where people used to come in and buy hundredweights and half hundredweights of coal. Mother lost a child through weighing up coal, which was hard work for a woman in those days. She died in 1939.

My father was principally involved with coal, but he started the timber side in 1926 and I joined the company in 1929. The Butt family also had a coal business down in Bowbridge. Another member of the family was Madame Pompadour, a hairdresser in King Street, and my cousin Audrey was a dance teacher and taught at Wycliffe College.

Ken Hill, born 1915

Townsend's Seed Mill was seriously damaged by fire in 1908, as shown in this picture. (Photograph courtesy of Howard Beard)

Townsend's seed mill

In 1933 I became an office boy at Townsend's, a farm, seed and food company which was on the site where Tesco is now. It was a large area, with a big mill building with its own railway siding and a turntable on the main rail, where the wagons could be brought and unloaded. After a while I was given the job of doing the ledgers; in those days everything was written out by hand, of course, and I entered ledgers and wrote out bills. I was about sixteen and still living at home in Slad. Then, Townsend's decided to make me a seed analyst and I found myself in the laboratory. I soon realised this was not for me and decided to look around for another job. In 1936 I started work at Gloster Aircraft Company at Brockworth.

Jim Fern, born 1918

Saturday morning jobs

Ward's coal was on the London Road where the solicitor's is now and they used to have this massive lump of coal outside. We used to have coal at home and I used to collect it for us and for a couple of ladies on Summer Street. It would take me all of Saturday morning to do it! I would have this trolley and go along Summer Street and down Hollow Lane to the Wharf (when what is now the car park was a proper working wharf) and I used to bring up the coal with this trolley – all the way back up and the buses going past me all the time. Alec Alder ran the wharf then and I started helping out; in return I got a lift back up the hill, so all I had to do was pull the trolley along Summer Street.

Geoff Franklin, born 1946

Delivering bread

I had a Saturday morning meat round from the butcher's shop at the Co-op in Chapel Street, run by a Mr Holder. I used to get one and sixpence. I then had a job going round in a van delivering bread with a Mr Jack Fern who was employed by Marsh and Watkins, who had a bakery in Bowbridge Lane, now replaced by houses. Mr Marsh was always well oiled and was always accompanied by a liver and white spaniel.

Reg Hancock, born 1925

Chimney sweeps and elvers

The milkman was Mr Close, who brought the milk in a churn and you had your jug outside. The baker was Mr Fern, the coalman was Mr Smart from Chalford, and the chimney sweep and street lamplighter was Mr Frank Burrows. When I was a young boy I could never understand how he could ride his bike at fifteen miles per hour with a rod on his shoulder and never seem to waver. He just had a way with him. The rod had a hook on the end for turning the lamps on at night and turning them off in the morning. When Mr Burrows came to our house as a chimney sweep, you had to move everything out, although you didn't really need to. He was so good, he'd ask if you wanted the soot to go up on the garden or otherwise he would take it away. It would be about half a crown to have the chimney done. Then there was Mr Winstone the ice cream man and, at the right time of year, a man would come round selling elvers: he would come round with his van and a great big enamel bath with live elvers in. They would be jumping up and down. I never liked them, but father did, so I would go and get a bowlful of elvers for sixpence. They were a delicacy but there were plenty of them in those days; they caught them down in the Severn.

Dennis Mason, born 1925

Travelling dentist

My father's memories go back much further than my mother's. He told me a story about a dentist who used to come to Stroud on a visiting basis to treat people. By repute, he brought with him a small number of musicians, who played brass instruments rather loudly in order to conceal the screams of people having teeth extracted.

Howard Beard, born 1943

A Red Cross volunteer

Before the war I was in the Red Cross. In those days there were no ambulances from the hospitals, only the Red Cross ambulances. When I was working at Townsend's I was allowed to go out on the ambulance, if it was

DENTAL NOTICE.

PAINLESS DENTISTRY

ADVICE FREE.

D. GORE BOODLE & Co., Ltd.

IN ATTENDANCE EVERY SATURDAY AT

(BOOT'S) RUSSELL STREET, STROUD.

(BRANCHES EVERYWHERE)

Surgery Hours:—10 a.m. to 6 p.m.
A LADY ALWAYS IN ATTENDANCE.

CROWN, BAR AND BRIDGE WORK GOLD AND OTHER FILLINGS
PRICES TO SUIT ALL PURSES
Our Extensive Practice is the result of excellence of our work.

We are now able to extract all Teeth (however badly decayed)
:: **WITHOUT THE SLIGHTEST PAIN** ::

BOODLE'S TEETH!

Extractions First Hour FREE.

Headquarters :-
Annandale House, GLOUCESTER.
—— Telephone 166 ——

Dentistry flyer. (Courtesy of Howard Beard)

an emergency, or if I was at home, it used to take me ten minutes on my pushbike to get to Stroud from Slad. The ambulance was kept in the Shambles: it was a Connor van, which had been converted. I used to go out with Philip Ford, the driver and either Reg Chapman, who was a blacksmith and had a forge down Gloucester Street, or the son of a printer in Stroud. We used to go out and collect people and take some of the poor old characters to the workhouse. The Red Cross office was where Woolworth's is now; it was on the top floor and we used to go there for lectures. Some of the Stroud doctors were involved and they carried out the tests.

Jim Fern, born 1918

Slipper baths, swimming pools and races on the canal

Where the precinct is now was a road which went down by the Green Dragon, and there was Tuck's Dance Hall, and further down there was slipper baths and a proper indoor swimming pool. It cost a couple of coppers to go in there: a chap called Clarence used to run it. He was a good swimmer. I used to go there and have a bath. We used to go swimming on the canal, down by the Bell in Wallbridge. There was a diving board round the side of Butts. We used to swim all the way up to the Black Bridge. They used to hold swimming races there too.

Reg Hancock, born 1925

Wallbridge, looking up towards the Bath Road, with the King's Arms on the left-hand side. This picture was taken before the acquisition of the Sea Scouts premises by Butts and the demolition of the pub and four cottages in the 1940s. Another house, later demolished at Wallbridge in the '70s, turned out to be a treasure trove of historical detail and the museum curator, Lionel Walrond, was able to rescue two rare shell-hood cupboards, as well as other artefacts and decorative items from the building, dated 1714. These can be seen at the Museum in the Park today.

Swimming pool down Bath Street

There used to be a swimming pool down Bath Street; we used to go there for swimming lessons. I can picture it now: it was a big room with tiled walls and all along the side there were little dressing rooms or cubicles, where you changed into your swimsuits.

Dorothy Harding, born 1922

Water polo on the canal

We used to have galas and play water polo on the canal. There was a men's section with a diving board, about twenty yards from the railway bridge, and a ladies' section further up. There were a lot of good swimmers. A fellow called Alan Baxter used to come down every morning, get up on the bridge and dive into the canal, even sometimes breaking the ice to dive in! He was a builder in Lansdown, all three brothers were in the building trade; they came to Butt's for lots of things.

Ken Hill, born 1915

Children weren't allowed in pubs

Years ago, between 1911 and 1933, my father's aunt kept the Golden Cross; her name was Taylor. My mother used to talk about how she met my father: he was staying with his aunt at the Golden Cross because he was from Yorkshire. Children weren't allowed in pubs in my day and women weren't either and then when they were, they weren't allowed in the bar with men.

Dorothy Harding, born 1922

The Golden Cross before 1928. The sign on the wall is Godsell & Sons Ltd, a brewery at Salmon Springs. Stroud Brewery acquired Godsell's, its main rival, in 1928. Note the postbox set into the wall of the pub. In later photographs it appears in the road.

The Smoke Room

My great-grandmother, Mrs Taylor, took the Golden Cross in Stroud in 1911. In those days it was not uncommon for a pub near a church to sell beer, stout and cider, but no spirits. She took this pub after running the Seven Stars at Ledbury because it was a beer house and her husband had been drinking too much whiskey! There was the bar and the Smoke Room: the pub was on a slope so the bottom part was the Smoke Room and the new part of the building was the bar, which opened out on to the top of Dudbridge Hill. In 1928, Godsell's Brewery merged with Stroud Brewery. Stroud, Nailsworth, Cainscross and Smith's Brewery at Brimscombe all became part of Stroud Brewery. Mr and Mrs Taylor's daughter, Mrs Bateman, took over the pub after her parents and stayed there until 1956.

A great many people would smoke different types of tobacco and one would say to another 'I can't smoke Bick's Empire, I can't smoke St Julien' and this sort of thing, but I remember one man used to smoke Royal Seal, which was a well-known tobacco at that time, in a yellow tin with a red seal on it. He would go over to the fireplace to get a spill out (we used to keep a box of spills on the mantelpiece) and he would light his pipe up and he would cough terrible when he'd first get the pipe going; clouds of smoke would come out of it and he would absolutely heave, his shoulders would go up and down and he'd cough terrible. One day he lit his pipe and father said 'Christ, Tom, why don't you give that pipe up?', and he replied 'It's me only bit of pleasure.'

David Russell, born 1939

Mrs Bateman, David Russell's grandmother, is sitting outside the Golden Cross in the late 1930s with two locals. A Red and White bus timetable is on the wall behind them.

Pigeons at the Oddfellows Arms

The Oddfellows Arms in Summer Street was about a quarter of a mile along on the right. A lot of people had pigeons there; people played darts, quoits and crib. It was very much a male society, very few women, and because children weren't allowed the majority of pubs had off sales: you would go into the entrance hall and there would be a sliding window to sell you sweets and crisps. Pubs were divided into little rooms and food wasn't served except for a pickled egg in a packet of crisps and a twist of salt.

Geoff Franklin, born 1946

Pigeon fanciers

I had pigeons when the war started, but mine weren't registered; I did not belong to a club, so the police destroyed them all. I used to get corn off other pigeon fanciers. In the 1940s the Stroud Pigeon Fanciers' Club used to meet at the Oddfellows Arms on Summer Street on a Friday night. The men used to take their pigeons there with their rings on: name, age and so on. They were registered in a book, put in baskets and sent off to race points to Tamworth, Chesterfield, Ripon, all over.

Reg Hancock, born 1925

Racing pigeons

Herbert Stanhope started the very early days of pigeon racing in this country. He lived in Hill House at the top of Stroud, on the way to Bisley. He was, and still is, very famous in pigeon racing. He produced a special strain of racing pigeon.

Stroud has always been a hotbed of pigeon racing. Stroud Valley Flying Club was set up in 1936 and was based at the Oddfellows Arms on Summer Street. They would take the pigeons down to Stroud station and they would be sent by rail to wherever, let off and

Oddfellows Arms, Summer Street, which closed in the early 1960s.

The same building today, virtually unrecognisable. (Photographs courtesy of Wilfred Merrett)

timed back in. I started racing pigeons in 1950 when we used to meet at the Railway Inn in Stroud (which is now closed), then in the late '50s at the Painswick Inn. The club is now based at the Stroud Rugby Club.

In the '30s Robert Perkins was an MP for Stroud and he had his own aeroplane – he

Stroud Brewery, c. 1930. This picture is taken from the Bell Inn and shows Rowcroft, going under the bridge, and Cheapside to the right. Drew's of Chalford built the brewery offices in 1901. The chimney was built in 1904 and demolished in 1967. The brewery itself was later demolished and was a rubbish site for years, until the Stroud and Swindon Building Society built their headquarters here, opening in March 1991. Stroud Brewery was started in 1873. At its height, in the 1930s, the company owned nearly 500 licensed premises. It was brewing 2,000 barrels a week and employed over 300 people when it finally shut down in 1967. (Photograph courtesy of Peckham's of Stroud)

used to fly from Hendon back to Oakridge. In the late '30s he set up a race to see whether he could beat the pigeons back to Oakridge in his plane. He donated a cup to the Flying Club to be awarded to the winner of the longest pigeon race.

Michael Mills, born 1932

No beer, cider only

There was a pear tree outside the Golden Cross. It was a type known as a strawberry burgundy and it was a round, hard pear with a red spot on and it was used to make perry, or pear cider, which you don't see much anymore (except of course that Babycham is

perry). There was a company called Robbins in Ebley in those days which survived until just after the war and we used to have home-made cider from there. When Robbins ceased trading we started having Weston's cider from Hereford, but it wasn't very well liked, so we changed to Bulmer's cider in about 1949.

In the pub, there was always plenty of cider, and, like many pubs, we would have only one barrel of beer a week. The allocation was very poor and we would put a sign up in the window which read 'No beer, cider only'. I remember Stroud Brewery was very stretched to supply beer to the pubs. I remember cider was sevenpence a pint and the beer was elevenpence and when the beer went up to a shilling that was terrible! I remember one man being annoyed about this and he said, 'Well, now the winter's come and the beer's gone up, I'm going to stay in nights and read a chapter out of the Bible,' and we never seen him any more, for weeks! That extra penny on the pint was the end. But I remember Grandmother saying it would be better for the change.

On a Sunday dinnertime, when we opened at twelve o'clock, the place was full; packed to the doors with working men having two or three pints before their Sunday dinner. At about twenty past twelve two women used to come down from Rodborough church, one was the choir mistress, and they always had their music bags and their black hats on, but when they got to the Golden Cross they always used to cross over and walk on the other side of the road, with their heads up.

David Russell, born 1939

The workhouse was awful

Before the war the workhouse, which is Stone Court now, was awful. People who used to stop there had to work; the ladies worked in the laundry. All the brick walls were dark green. The poor kiddies marched down to school at Parliament Street in their blue and white dresses. Some went on and some stayed, and lots of children were born in the workhouse. It was a dreadful place; should never have been allowed.

Dorothy Harding, born 1922

The neglected people

The workhouse as I knew it as a youngster symbolised the tragic side of life. We lived only a few hundred yards from it and I can see them now, on a Tuesday night when they had fire drill: the engines would arrive and I can see them lowering the stretchers down, to make sure they could cope if there was a fire. The workhouse people were those who were down on their luck and those on hard times; the neglected people. We don't have a workhouse now; that symbolises to me just how much we have progressed.

Dennis Mason, born 1925

Poor old characters

In *Cider with Rosie*, Laurie Lee speaks of Joseph and Hannah Brown who were taken to the workhouse against their will because they couldn't cope. They used to segregate the women from the men. The men wore tough suiting and they did jobs out in the community. The women were also somewhat employed. We used to take poor old characters there who had nowhere else to go and were sick. We used to go out in the ambulance and find them, sometimes up little lanes where we had to reverse back down to get out. I sat inside, I didn't drive, and we would take them up to the workhouse, or to the hospital. We then had to carry them out on an iron stelray stretcher, up the side of the building, into wards, which were spartan: bare walls, wooden floors with knots showing up where they were so worn. The poor old characters watching them come in probably thought this was the most exciting thing they had seen for ages. These people would often stay in the workhouse until they passed on. There was no way out.

Jim Fern, born 1918

Sent to the workhouse

When the Americans came to town during the Second World War they were stationed in what was once the workhouse, the place where men wore off-white corduroy trousers, which are fashionable today but were frowned on then; the women wore aprons. They did washing, ironing and other tasks. Men did gardening and broke up stones; there was like a quarry round the back. I remember one family whose father left his wife and five children; she became ill and they were all sent to the workhouse. When she got better she did manage to get herself out and get her children back.

Reg Hancock, born 1925

The Baptist church

I was brought up at the Baptist chapel in Stroud. My parents had been attending there since before I was born. When I was a youngster the organist was a lady called Ethel Brinkworth. Along with her sister, she ran a small private school in Folly Lane. By that time she had been the church organist for fifty years, but the problem was that she had become blind as she got older. She still played all the hymns in the Baptist hymnbook – and played them beautifully – but she didn't know when the last verse of each hymn had begun. My mother's job was to nudge her during it so that she didn't launch herself into another verse that didn't exist.

My mother's family had been Baptists for generations. They were Nailsworth folk originally. The chapel at Shortwood had been founded as far back as 1715 and, at one time, had been amongst the largest half-dozen or so Baptist communities in the country.

At the chapel in Stroud, when I was a boy, there was a dynamic minister called the Reverend Tugwell. He was a very good orator and increased the size of the congregation there considerably. I used to attend morning church, afternoon Sunday school and the evening service. That was what was expected and we all did it.

I occasionally see friends who run choirs in other churches. These days most places are struggling to find enough people to sing, but it's wasn't very long ago that you would find choirs of thirty or forty people or more. At the Baptist church there was also a women's

The Baptist chapel in John Street, c. 1907. (Photograph courtesy of Howard Beard)

meeting, there were Christian Endeavour clubs and various other activities.

My father signed 'the pledge' back in the 1920s and he kept his promise consistently until a family wedding in the late 1950s, when he was tempted with a glass of Austrian white wine, which he rather enjoyed! My mother was horrified that he had broken the pledge but, after that, both he and I would enjoy the occasional glass.

Howard Beard, born 1943

Church was a way of life

We were brought up to go to chapel every Sunday morning, to Sunday school in the afternoon and then to chapel again in the evening. We attended the old Congregationalist church, which was situated off Middle Street, in what is now called Chapel Street. It used to be so full and there wasn't enough room for everyone to attend both services. As a result, they built Bedford Street Congregational church to take the overflow. In the 1970s the whole picture changed: we were down to about seven members and we had no alternative but to close down. We linked up with the Bedford Street church and they demolished the old chapel.

Church, for us, was a way of life and the Sunday school was absolutely thriving; Mr Robert Peer was the superintendent and other teachers included Mr Harry Nichols, who worked at James and Owens in Russell Street, which is now in London Road. He was never seen without a rose in his buttonhole. Other officers were my uncle, Mr Reg Griffin, and my auntie, who was in the choir; we were all involved in the chapel. Everybody went in those days – it was a family gathering.

When we started Sunday school, it was in a room off the main church and the dear lady in charge was a Mrs Annie Coffin. We sat on little chairs and we would sing, 'You in your small corner and I in mine'.

We have many churches in Stroud: the Cotswold Playhouse on Parliament Street used to be the home of the Primitive Methodist church, which was another branch of the Methodist cause. During the war, their organist went into the Navy, so they had no one there to play the music. Eventually the church closed and is now a theatre.

In Rodborough, the Tabernacle was the leading place for Methodist worship in the whole country in the eighteenth century, and in Lower Street you had the Castle Street Methodist church, which closed down and is now flats. Just up the hill you've got the Salvation Army Citadel in Acre Street: it is Britain's oldest surviving Methodist chapel and one of the very few in the country which is octagonal shaped. Next door we have the Plymouth Brethren meeting room. Stroud's parish church is St Laurence's, which is very well attended, as is Holy Trinity by the hospital.

Dennis Mason, born 1925

The Primitive Methodist chapel, c. 1908. The building became the Cotswold Playhouse in the 1950s. (Photograph courtesy of Howard Beard)

Holy Trinity

The church played more part in your lives those days. Mum used to take us to Holy Trinity for the occasional service. The vicar was called Mr Eynon. Mothering Sunday was a great service: every year, Sutton's, the florist whose shop was halfway up Middle Street, used to supply a pot plant for every child. In the service each child would go up to the altar to take a plant which they would then present to their mother; either a hyacinth or a primula. We used to go to Sunday school in Trinity Rooms and we used to have Brownies there too. There used to be a stage in there and they used to put on Harvest Suppers and people used to do performances and monologues and things like that. There was a club there called Wives' Club or Young Wives, which was an equivalent of the WI, which Mum used to go to on a Monday night. Where Weavers Croft is now, there was a field where we used to have Trinity fête and there were pony rides and skiffle groups and stalls; it used to be great fun.

Pam Spokes, born 1949

The Stroud Show

I remember the Stroud Shows when they were held in Fromehall Park Road. There were lots of floats and nearly every works had a jazz band; it was lovely in those days. The parade used to set off from Field Road, near the hospital, and make its way down to Fromehall Park. The Show eventually became too big for Fromehall Park and in 1952 it moved to Stratford Park instead. In the early days it used to be a three-day event and farmers would bring their animals and livestock along to show, but after a while they made it just the one day.

Dorothy Harding, born 1922

Above and below: Floats for the Stroud Show parade down Middle Street, 1954.

Everyone took part

Holloway's of Brick Row, Hill Paul's of Cheapside, Strachan's of Bath Road and all the villages and streets entered jazz bands in the Stroud Show. The parade would start at Field Road by the Hospital and go through the town to Stratford Park for judging. There were rabbit shows, bird shows, dog shows; lorries would be decorated and carry Snow White and the Seven Dwarves and all sorts of acts and scenery.

Reg Hancock, born 1925

The fair at Fromehall Park

The Stroud Show was at Fromehall Park every year from about 1935 and then every year until 1952 when it moved to Stratford Park. It was a very big event and caused great excitement. There were a huge assortment of vehicles that brought the fair to town: Roger's Fair of Chipping Sodbury had a large number of American lorries which had a job to get into Fromehall Park because they were so big. When they got to the Golden Cross with three wagons on, they would unhitch them and take them in one at a time. They also had a couple of Scammells and an American MAC left-hand drive and sometimes we could get a ride on that into the ground. The fairground people would often give us free rides in exchange for a few Woodbines.

David Russell, born 1939

Father drove a float

There was always a huge carnival for the Stroud Show; I remember it being held at Stratford Park. Apart from the huge arts and crafts and produce tents, what I really remember are the floats. My father used to drive one and he would spend ages polishing his lorry, ready to drive it through the town. The parade was so long it seemed to go on forever. But in the '50s that's what happened. People don't do that sort of thing now. It was unsophisticated and very time-consuming, but people did have much more time then – there was no telly!

Pam Spokes, born 1949

Motorcycle football at Fromehall Park

Other events were held at Fromehall Park, including boxing before and after the war. They used to set up a boxing ring in front of that grandstand. There was motorcycle football, which was quite a big thing just after the war. They even had a motorcycle football league. Tom Powles, who kept the Targets, up the Bisley Road, was a big motorcycle football fan and the matches they played used to draw large crowds.

David Russell, born 1939

Stroud motorcycle football team pictured in the late 1930s. (Photograph courtesy of Michael Mills)

Circus elephants at Cainscross on their way to Victory Park in 1954.

The circus comes to town

The circus came to Stroud a few times. They brought some elephants along from Stroud station and up the Bath Road. They would give you a poster to put up and we were each given a free ticket to go. We did well.

David Russell, born 1939

Elephants at the station

The circus used to come to Stroud – to Fromehall Park and also to Victory Park at Ebley. We went down to watch them take the elephants off the train at the station and walk them all the way to Victory Park.

Dorothy Harding, born 1922

two
Childhood

Home-made rice pudding

I was born in 1925 and mother gave up work and became a housewife. Her speciality was her home-made rice puddings: my sister and I always had to take it in turns to run our fingers round the outside of the pie dish. Lovely!

Monday was washday, there were no machines and the boiler was part of the house, built of stone, a good old copper. On Sunday night dad would lay the fire under the copper so it was all ready to go off on Monday morning. The toilet was outside, which wasn't very nice if it was pouring with rain, and we had no bathroom at all, so we bathed in front of the fire once a week, and you always made sure you washed your hair in rainwater. At the top of the garden Dad had his workshop, which eventually became the home of the motorbike: a BSA Bantam.

Dennis Mason, born 1925

Happy days

In 1929 I started at Parliament Street Church of England School in Stroud, aged three. I left at fourteen. They were happy days: playing marbles in the gutter on the way home, asking men on their way home from work if they had any cigarette cards I could have. There were usually fifty to a set, so it was a challenge, and I would swap among the other children if I had any doubles. Woodbines were fourpence, Players sixpence and there were cards in both. Kensitas was really the best, but they were not in the working man's reach; they contained silk flags and the like.

Everyone had time for each other and doors were open and people spoke, not always kindly, if you stepped out of line. As we grew up we all had a spell in the garden, weeding and digging, planting and grass cutting.

Pocket money was earned, it was not a right, with errands for aunts, uncles, grandmothers and grandfathers. I remember the boys' and girls' club in the old chapel: table tennis, quoits, rings, snakes and ladders and draughts, under supervision. On a Monday night I went to the Penny Bank and Co-operative Stores in Chapel Street – that was to encourage saving.

Reg Hancock, born 1925

Everyone knew each other

We moved to No. 4 The Granvilles, Bisley Road, from a flat in Brimscombe when I was about three. My father was from Bristol and my mother was from Croydon in Surrey and they would never have met if not for the great leveller – the war. I remember Stroud as a community where you knew people and people knew you. Bisley Road was 'posh' in those days; we had a huge late-Victorian semi. Mum had been left a legacy, which was how we afforded it. We were next to some redundant allotments, which was great because we used to play on them. There were slow-worms and overgrown raspberry bushes. In 1959 the builders got hold of it and put up some more semis.

Pam Spokes, born 1949

Out all day

One of the most popular spots when we were youngsters was the Targets, situated between where we lived at the top of Stroud and Lypiatt. We would either take our cricket bats or our bows and arrows, pretending to be Robin Hood, and we would spend our time up at Snakeshole, turning over the big stones to see if we could find any snakes. Or we would spend our time in the bluebell wood, building dens up in the trees and then coming home laden with bluebells; you wouldn't do that now. You went out at ten in the morning and came home at five in the evening and had your tea and there was no worries.

Dennis Mason, born 1925

Pam Spokes as a little girl in 1956.

Never any badness

Out of school time we used to play mothers and fathers and schools; I used to pretend to be a schoolteacher and sometimes we'd put on a pantomime. We'd go along the Targets and there used to be loads of butterflies, which we'd catch with a net. We'd take a picnic, some sandwiches and pop and go along Beeches Wood, which comes down into Strawberry Fields and Summer Street. That was always nice and you could go right along into Swifts Hill, which is along at Slad. We always went out and played, we weren't frightened; there was never any badness, not a ha'porth of badness, even when the American forces were at the workhouse during the Second World War.

Dorothy Harding, born 1922

The rough end of Stroud

My dad came from Stroud; my mum came from Cinderford. I don't know how they met. Evelyn was my mum and Harold was my dad, but he was always known as Titch (he was a bit 'vertically challenged'). Dad was from a Stroud family, born and bred. He used to cut all our hair, which was dreadful because it really was the old pudding basin cut, the girls as well! And he always used to mend all our shoes. As you can imagine, trying to keep ten children in clothes and shoes was quite a feat.

Our dad was a builder's labourer all his life; he worked for Savage's, an Ebley firm. Our mum used to work; she would get up and do cleaning from six to eight in the morning and then come home to get the kids off to school, and then go back in the evening to do more cleaning. They were really hard-working folk. They started their married life in Summer Street, which was the rough end of Stroud.

We had nowhere else to play but we had Target woods and the Daisy Bank and Snakeshole behind the Target pub. Kids were always milling around in those days; playing in the woods, building swings, and on those banks in the summer it was laden with snakes,

there were loads of them there. Then there was Rodborough Common and Minchinhampton. We loved fishing and the Stroudwater canal was good for that; it didn't cost you a lot of money to do and it was fun.

Geoff Franklin, born 1946

Collecting butterflies

I used to go bird-nesting. All the boys in the village did. It's against the law now, but it wasn't then. I also collected butterflies at one stage. Rather sadly, my butterfly collection was put away one winter and, by the spring, the moths had eaten them – a kind of insect cannibalism! All that was left was the bodies and the pins. I remember too, as a child, going up into Thrupp woods and collecting armfuls of bluebells, again not allowed today. I also used to collect holly at Christmas.

Then there was the canal: in abandoned locks you could lie down on the stone edging, put

Summer Street, *c.* 1910. (Photograph courtesy of Howard Beard)

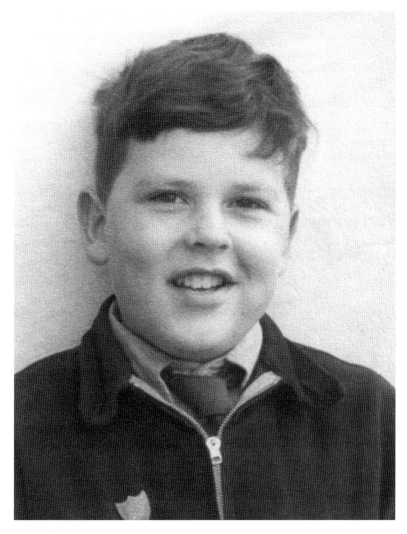

Howard Beard aged eleven.

your hand into the water and hook newts out from amongst the weed. We also used to take jam jars along and catch minnows. When I was older I caught roach in the canal. Moorhens used to nest out on platforms of weed and we used to see if we could climb out along willow branches to get an egg. Once I found a duck's nest with its pale blue eggs. When we were young none of us swam, either! I didn't learn to swim until I had lessons at Marling School.

Howard Beard, born 1943

Nine in the family

My Dad was a Swindon man and when he married my mum she was from Gloucester, and my grandfather on my mum's side was chief warden of Gloucester Cathedral. There was five born in Swindon but I was born in Gloucester in 1906. The family moved from Gloucester to Dursley and then to Ebley. There was three more born in Ebley, two boys and a girl, so there was nine of us altogether: Frank, Cisy (but her name was Florence),

Fred, Harold, Lily, Edith, Harry, Bert and Babs – well, she was Ethel – but she was the last one to be born so we called her Babs.

When we lived in Ebley we were poor, but we were always brought up to say please and thank you, because our parents in those days were very strict. You never saw the children that lived in Ebley running around; they always had to walk, especially on a Sunday. We went to Sunday school in the morning and Sunday school in the afternoon.

Edie Lee, born 1906

Arnold's fish and chips

Stroud had a mobile fish and chip van that used to visit Thrupp. It was owned by Arnold's, whose shop near the Cross has been demolished now. This brown-painted fish and chip van used to come up the valley to Thrupp, park at the top of the little lane that led down to Hope Mills and a bell would announce that it had arrived. If you didn't hear the bell, it didn't matter because you could smell it anyway! The van had a little chimney on it. We would hurry down and buy three penn'orth of chips: that was usually the order of the day.

Howard Beard, born 1943

Summer Street antics

There used to be a police station on the corner of Summer Street and the Bisley Road; policemen in them days were different to how they are now. At the bottom of Hollow Lane, on the right, was the Scout Hut. We always hung around in great gangs of kids and once a group of kids decided to throw fireworks over to annoy the Scouts. One of the policemen heard the fireworks and came running down from the police station in the pitch black; he caught hold of me and said I was throwing the fireworks. Of course, I never

had any money to buy fireworks! I was terrified but I was had up under the Explosives Act when I was about nine. I was taken to Stroud Court, which was an enormous embarrassment to the family and I was fined about ten shillings!

A lot of other antics used to go on too. From Summer Street, if you walk to the end of Summer Crescent, there's a place called Woodside; you could walk up in to the wood there and come out on Swifts Hill. Halfway along was Horns Farm, which had a row of plum trees. Course, the closer the trees were to the wood, the more they were in the shade and the plums weren't quite so nice, so it was only the bravest who went further down to the house to get the better plums. The ridiculous thing was that in our garden we had plum trees and apple trees, but they were no way near as nice as those pinched from down the road.

Geoff Franklin, born 1946

The Daisy Bank

When I was young, we used to go out and play all day in the fields. We would go up that track past the Daisy Bank, past the second bit of the graveyard, down to the weighhouse stream and up into the woods where there was an old quarry; it used to be called Silverthorne Farm. We used to play down by the canal and the River Frome. In the Daisy Bank there were swings and a see-saw and an appalling concrete slide. I always think that it might never have been finished; it should have had a metal lining, but we used to throw mud on it and slide down it. Our parents used to get so cross when we came home filthy with our clothes torn. And then in the summer when the grass was dry, we used to take up cardboard boxes and slide on the grass and you could really get up some speed. We used to catch lizards out of the wall which backs on to the cemetery and take a handful of lizards home. I remember people being bitten by adders too.

Pam Spokes, born 1949

Brought up in a pub

My grandmother brought my brother and I up at the pub, the Golden Cross, because our mother died just after we were born and our father was away at sea. We were twins. She had come to Stroud because her daughter's husband, Mr Bateman, was a butcher at the Co-op at Cainscross. So, my maternal grandparents were called Bateman; my grandfather died just before the war.

I can just remember my paternal grandparents, the Russell's, who were from Thrupp. Mr Russell lived till he was about eighty and he would not allow Mrs Russell to have a gas cooker. This was not uncommon; there were a lot of people who saw other people gassed in the First World War and they were anti-gas. The week after he died, sometime in the late 1940s, she had a gas cooker put in and she told everyone how wonderful it was to do the potatoes in half an hour, instead of having to boil them over the fire. They had a black chain over the fire with a pot and it used to take hours.

We had the same time type of fireplace at the Golden Cross: an open fire with an oven on the side. In those days, my grandmother used to cook part of the meals in the oven and we used to have to blacklead the fireplace on Saturday mornings; that's one of those jobs which is not really done nowadays. We used to keep firebricks in there: we used to wrap them up in brown paper and take them up to bed with us at night as hot water bottles.

David Russell, born 1939

Mrs Bateman in 1955, with darts player Percy Lambert and the only darts cup the Golden Cross ever won.

Cider-making in Ebley

I had four brothers and two sisters; there were eight of us but one little boy died when he was very young. I'm the second youngest and I have only got my sister left. There was John Victor, Albert Edward (everyone called him Nutty; he was always getting up our nut trees and picking the nuts before they were ripe); then there was Joe who died when he was five years old (mother never told me why and I never pressed it), then the twins, Donald and Ronald, Alice, then me, and Patricia, the youngest. We had a wonderful time together and a happy family life. During the Great War my mother worked at Horsfall's, the launderer's, prior to getting married. My father, John Curtis, did a job at Marling and Evans and when he came home he did another three or four hours every night, cider-making with three orchards full of apples and pears. We sold our stuff to local shops. We all did our share; the boys did the haymaking in the orchard and I helped mother with the washing and ironing.

We preserved a lot of our own fruit: loads of red, black and white currants, strawberries, raspberries and loganberries. We always went mushrooming: my father used to get me up at about six in the morning and off we would go and we would come back and have breakfast. When we went blackberrying we would be away all day. We took baskets, bowls – anything – and we went up the Rough Bank towards Selsey. It was quite a way, but through the fields from Ebley it was not so far. We ate most of the blackberries before we got back to the house and we used to wash our faces in the stream. Mother bottled the blackberries and made gorgeous apple and blackberry pies. To make the preserves, the fruit first went in cold water and then she popped them in the oven until we could see the water bubbling, then we pulled them out, quickly screwed them down and left them.

We produced cider and perry too (pear cider). We put the apples through a mincer to get crushed, we strained them, and the juice from all the crushed apples would go down a chute into a big barrel. A horse would go round and round to work a turning mechanism, then it was put into coconut matting and folded like an envelope and put in a press, and more juice would come out along a chute, through a strainer and be put into barrels. My father and uncles would bottle it. We took all our bottles to local shops on a horse and cart, up Foxmoor Lane to Mr Robbins and sometimes to the Coach and Horses. We had six pigs and we had our own milk from the cows.

Holly Tree Cottage, Ebley, 1936. From left to right, back row: Mabel with dog, Fred (Alice's husband), Pat. Front row: Jack, Granny Curtis, Mother.

The milk didn't go through a cooler, or even a strainer.

We would put the other apples in rows, on brown paper in the attic, not touching each other and they kept the whole of the summer through: Cox's Orange Pippins, Blenheims, Russets and Worcestershires. We had Williams pears, Russet pears and one which we called a Barn Pear. The Williams pear was the one we made the perry with. The pears would go soft quickly; if they weren't ripe when we picked them we put them in a drawer and they would ripen within a couple of days.

May Bell Dullea, born 1925

Rugby at Victory Park

My first appearance on a rugby field was at the age of nine. I went along to Victory Park, Cainscross, one evening in September at the start of the season. We were a motley group of boys: the ball was chucked up and everyone went for it; I remember seeing stars! There was I, on the ground with ten kids on top of me, right at the bottom if the pile and I was told I was too young for the game. I was wearing my father's Gloucester Victoria shirt, I remember it smelt of mothballs. The big attraction for most of the boys was the bun-fight that followed with the gallons of ginger beer in a back room at the White Horse Inn, situated on what was then the actual cross-roads at Cainscross. Stroud RFC became the first major rugby club in the country to start a Colts section at Fromehall Park in 1955. I was its first chairman but John Garner and Brian Dainty did the real work, on a week-by-week basis.

John V. Smith, born 1926

Stroud, to me, was wonderful

Before I had my Saturday jobs I went to the pictures in the morning at the Gaumont. It was fourpence to get in: cowboys and indians, *The Undersea Kingdom*, all that wonderful stuff. We also went fishing in the canal with a penny net from Backhouse's on Middle Street: we'd take a jam jar and get sticklebacks, newts and minnows.

At the age of eleven I would go along to Target Woods and make bows and arrows from nut trees and smoke petiwine – that was plentiful and you could swing on it too, like Tarzan. We made dens and had rivalries with boys from Horns Road and Lower Street.

Stroud to me was wonderful; we could get a bag of scrumps from Bradshaw's the fish and chip shop on the Cross for one penny, and we would call into Tucks' cake shop and ask for stale cakes and get a bagful for a penny: cream horns, doughnuts, Chelseas, cream slices and lardies.

Reg Hancock, born 1925

Saturday mornings at Daniels

I didn't know Lionel Daniels personally, as he died in the January of the year in which I was born. My father, John Daniels, was in the works at Lightpill and, as a seven-year-old, I used to go down with him on Saturday mornings. His office was on a mezzanine floor and from there I could see all the cranes and quite a bit of activity: lines of lathes and machinery, which was fascinating to watch. I also remember the foundry, with the sand, which had a very distinctive smell: I always liked that smell because I associated it with my father. I can remember seeing some very large boilers with a very small hole, through which a man had to climb with a torch to clean inside. I can remember the cranes and the big machines.

Juliana Daniels, born 1958

The Photo Electric Playhouse, c. 1910. (Photograph courtesy of Howard Beard)

Stroud's cinemas

Stroud's earliest cinema was along Lansdown. It was called the Photo Electric Playhouse. Spot Walker ran this cinema in around 1910. Old postcards show how he tried to encourage people to attend by dressing up his regular youngsters as cowboys and indians. They would then parade around the town to persuade others to come along. He would cover two small boys in bootblack, put feathers and grass skirts on them and pretended they were African natives. He called them Timbucone and Timbuctwo. Spot's cinema was later used as a dance school.

There were two cinemas in Stroud when I was young, the Gaumont and the Ritz. The Ritz burnt down in 1961. I was meant to be revising for my A-levels at the time and I was just returning early from my girlfriend's house when I saw the fire and took time off to watch it. The shopping precinct by the side of where Woolworth's is today was built where the Ritz once stood. When I was a small boy I used to go to both the Gaumont and the Ritz regularly: they were very crowded in those days. We didn't have many other forms of entertainment.

Howard Beard, born 1943

Saturday morning pictures at the Gaumont

We used to go to Saturday morning pictures at the Gaumont; that was back in the days when they used to have talent shows and there were a lot of skiffle groups in them days, with the washboard and the tea chest. It started off with cartoons, then 'Lily', then interval time for you to buy your ice-lollies, or whatever, and then they had the serial, which was an endless thing. Downstairs was sixpence and upstairs was ninepence and I could never work this out. We used to get sevenpence to go to the pictures:

The opening of the Gaumont by Jessie Matthews in 1931. (Photograph courtesy of Peckham's of Stroud)

sixpence to get in and a penny packet of bits from Granny Ball. We would eat the bits in the cinema and afterwards go for a bag of 'scrumps' from Arnold's chip shop. That was the broken bits of batter off the fish. Delicious!

Geoff Franklin, born 1946

Saturday night at the movies

Every Saturday night whenever possible, my mother, my sister and me would catch the bus at five past five from the bottom of Belmont Road down to Stroud. We either went to the Gaumont, which was opened by Jessie Matthews and Sunny Hale in 1931, or to the Ritz, which didn't open until 1939. It was mainly the Gaumont. We would catch a bus home at about half past eight. You would stand for the National Anthem then there was a stampede for the buses.

Dennis Mason, born 1925

During the interval

Along Cainscross there are some new buildings on the main road now, but there's a stone building opposite the Co-op which used to be the Old Bank Picture House. It was a penny to go in, but we used to have to take it in turns because Mum couldn't afford to get us all in. When we came out we always used to have a bag of sweets. Someone used to do a turn in between the films and once, when it was my turn to go, a young man came out in a navy-blue suit and a flower in his buttonhole and he sang:

Always wear a flower in your coat,
When you go to meet your girl.
Something smart,
To captivate her heart and send her in a whirl.
She won't notice the colour of your clothes,
If you're wearing a pink or a rose.
So, always wear a flower in your coat,
When you go to meet your girl.

Edie Lee, born 1906

The Ritz, c. 1939. (Photograph courtesy of Peckham's of Stroud)

Living like barons

We ate what was available or what they had plenty of: pork or veal and there was always a block of corned beef that was used for corned beef hash and corned beef sandwiches on a Saturday night. There were a lot of poor families around, but we lived in a pub so we were like barons, because we could get anything. My grandmother had quite a thing going: people would bring rabbits in for ten Woodbines so we always had plenty of rabbit stew. We had all our own chickens and plenty of eggs. I remember at Easter Gran used to tell us to go down and tell the chickens to lay us some pink eggs: so we had these pink eggs and I was quite amazed at why they only laid pink eggs at Easter – until I got a bit older and found this bottle of cochineal in the cupboard.

David Russell, born 1939

Car trips with father

We acquired a car – an old Austin 10, ED 7964 – when I was about eight or nine years old. My father had learned to drive back in 1923, when he was working for his father's building firm. He had driven all sorts of vehicles. My grandfather had some nice cars back in the 1930s but, when the war came, these were disposed of. Once we had a car, this made us more mobile. My father was a creature of habit and, every Saturday morning after work at Hoffman's factory, he would come back for his lunch and, in the afternoon, we would go out in the car. We went somewhere within about twenty or thirty miles, to have a look around a town and have tea. My father reckoned that a pound note would see us through the afternoon: that would be enough to put some petrol in the car and also buy tea for four of us at a café. The car had old-fashioned pop-up indicators. On one occasion we stopped in Russell Street to post a letter. I nipped out rather too quickly to do it and ripped off an indicator as I did so! I was not popular that day.

Howard Beard, born 1943

Cainscross Garage in the 1920s, previously The Old Bank Picture House. (Photograph courtesy of Mike Goodenough)

Whitsuntide in Ebley

At Whitsuntide there was a brass band and we were all in our finery, we came from the chapel and we walked up Chapel Lane into Ebley as far as Cainscross and at the crossroad we sang hymns and then came back along the road to Ebley. We all had Whitsuntide 'bosses,' a flower which grows in a bush, round like a ball with little white flowers. We sang hymns as we went along. We used to go to people's gardens and bless them: Propagation Day I think it was called. We had races in the meadow and there were prizes all ready to give us if we won. We had a carnival, which followed behind the band, and a Whitsuntide tea. I made my own costume and won first prize.

May Bell Dullea, born 1925

Horns Road football team

Where I lived on Horns Road, we had our own football team and we played up Bisley Road. We played 'friendlies' and eventually most of us played for Stroud Trinity. But I had an ankle injury and the last game I had was up at Chalford. I loved cricket most of all though.

Ken Hill, born 1915

The rosehip collector

When I was a child we were encouraged to go out into the countryside and collect the rosehips that the manufacturers of rosehip syrup required. We were told that we could get three old pence a pound for this – half a week's pocket money – so it was worth doing. We were also given badges; I've still got my rosehip collector's badge.

Howard Beard, born 1943

The Horns Road football team, 1929/30. From left to right, back row: Eric Field, Lionel Brown, ? Wyn, Doug Powis, Ewart Weaving, Bob Webb, Lionel Hobson, Ken Hill. Middle row: Darrell Russell, Claude Mather, Jimmy Mutton; Front row: ? Wheatley, Frank Paul, Doug Harmer.

Ken Hill in 2004. (Photograph by Peta Bunbury)

Howard Beard in 2004.

three

School
Days

Parliament Street

We lived in Belmont Road at the top of Stroud and the nearest school was Parliament Street, which was about half a mile down the hill. It was a lovely school, very small. We used to go home to dinner, then back to school and then home again afterwards. The headmaster was a Mr Smith and other teachers were a Mr Barrett, a Miss Roberts, a Miss Price and a Miss Lawrence. At the age of eleven I did the school certificate and went to the Marling School. Parliament Hill School is now the Registry Office; where we used to play now provides a perfect backdrop for the photographer to take his pictures!

Dennis Mason, born 1925

Dennis Mason as a schoolboy.

School days were very enjoyable

I went to school at Parliament Street. It's closed now and is a Registry Office – they have built the new school up the road, on the fields where we used to go for sports. My school days were very enjoyable; we never had any bullying or nothing. There was never any wickedness of any kind. We learnt more in a day than what the kiddies learn in a week now and there was much more discipline. I remember the teacher had a ruler, which she would tap your hand with. I liked geography and I loved arithmetic and I liked history, especially the Romans, Greeks and Egyptians. Great stories! My friends were Pauline Daniels, Betty Howlett and Renee Wheatley.

Dorothy Harding, born 1922

Bunch of hooligans

My oldest sister is Maureen, then there's Margaret, Jean, Val, Mary and Penny, Tony, Geoff, Clifford and Robert. We all started off at Parliament Street School. I started at the Infants down below the main school. I always remember having to have a sleep in the afternoon on one of those little fold-up camp beds. I remember the headmaster, Mr Smith, or 'Corry' Smith as we used to call him, and a Mrs Wyatt who was the playground attendant. I realise now that we were a bunch of hooligans and we needed a dragon around us. She probably wasn't all that bad!

We used to have little thirds of a pint of milk at break time and we used to have to go to the clinic, which is down below Stroud Hospital, and see the nit nurse; she was there for donkey's years, this woman. We also used to get cod liver oil and malt, which came in a cardboard tub and was like thick toffee, and concentrated orange too.

Mr Click was the truancy officer. If you didn't come to school Mr Click would be round to see where you'd got to. I remember

Mr Click well! The truancy people had their hands full with the Summer Street lot. On reflection, it was a tough old time, but in some ways it was a lot less complicated because nobody had nothing and everybody was in the same boat; everybody struggled.

Geoff Franklin, born 1946

Rodborough County School

My brother and I went to Rodborough County School and if you didn't pass the 11-plus you stayed at that school until you were fifteen. Mr Foster was the headmaster then and Mrs Holder was his assistant – she was very religious. There were three people in the class whose families kept a pub: David Wilson's family had the Bedford Arms in Stroud, Diane Knight's family had the Anchor and we had the Golden Cross. Mrs Holder disliked pubs immensely and we were always in her bad books. In those days, at the end of each term you did a written test on religion and I remember I disliked this because I could never remember anything; I just wanted to get back to the pub and play darts or quoits. We didn't pass our 11-plus and we stayed at Rodborough School till we were fifteen; we were the last people to do that because when I went in the army at eighteen to do National Service, they built the new school at Paganhill, Archway, which became the new secondary modern and everybody went there.

David Russell, born 1939

Castle Street Girls' School

We arrived, aged seven, at Castle Street Girls' School, mainly from the Infants' School up the road. The school, also known as the Black Boy School because of a blackamoor figure on the striking clock, was a tall building at the top of town. It was guarded by thick, iron railings at the front where little boys got their heads stuck, an old chapel to the side and thinner railings at the bottom of the playing field. It was a school of evocative smells: of old wood, warm comforting fumes from the stoves, mice, and, through the windows, the sweet headiness of June or the metallic smell of impending snow in January.

The flooring was bare, wooden board throughout, and splinters were part of the school day. The toilets were outside, bitterly cold in winter, with icicles draped from cisterns too frozen to flush. There were washbasins indoors, but no hot water and permanently damp roller towels, which were good to swing on. Heating was provided by large, black cast-iron stoves, one in each classroom with a tortoise motif and 'slow but sure' on top. Iron rails protected already chilblained fingers from reaching the hot stoves, which we crowded round on cold days, reluctantly dragging ourselves away when ordered to our desks.

Parents and children alike were all in awe of Miss F.R. Peacock (Fanny Peacock to us girls), headmistress and form teacher of the top class. She was of indeterminate age, though to us she was ancient, her style entrenched firmly in the 1930s. She favoured short-sleeved linen dresses from that period, buttoned down the front, in dull mustard or sage green; wore black Minnie Mouse shoes and no stockings; always bare-legged. She looked the same, winter or summer, and wore an intimidating calf-length black coat in winter, which made her appear like a crow if she went outside. Her hair was cut in a severe bob, straight, with a huge hairgrip on one side. We would be viewed piercingly from over the top of her horn-rimmed spectacles. She was strict, direct, an excellent teacher, sometimes fun, and she terrified us all.

Our day would formally begin with assembly in the upstairs hall. We would stand silently in rows as Miss Peacock swept in with 'Good

Castle Street Girls School, Christmas 1958. From left to right, back row: Sheila Andrew, Jennifer Hunt, Christine Buckle, -?-, -?-, Brenda Wheatley, Ann Price, Jane Elliman, Susan Iles, Mary Tipple, Yvonne Williams, Susan Harrison. Middle row: -?-, Marilyn Price, Sally Laming, Janet Gardner, Sheila Jones, Davina Johnson, Julie Lasbury, Jennifer Watts, Valerie Cook, Margaret Iles. Front row: Caroline Comben, Susan Andrews, Victoria Thomas, Jennifer Gardner, Susan Marley, Heather Foreshoe, Nancy Evans, Pamela Spokes, Stephanie Sims, Pricilla Bird, Elaine Turner, Vivienne Hayward, Margaret Brown, Diana Barker.

morning girls.' Latecomers sliding in had to stand by the door in full view of the rest of the school, uneasily waiting to be dealt with later. Miss Peacock would belt out a hymn tune on the rickety piano, perching on an old bentwood chair. We were only issued with hymnbooks once a week, on Wednesdays, when we had hymn practice. On the other four days they stayed in the cupboard, and we were expected to know the words to whichever hymn she chose. Woe betide us if we faltered, say, in the third verse of 'To be a pilgrim'.

We must have followed some sort of curriculum, I suppose; our learning was certainly heavily biased towards the three R's. Much was learned by rote; the sounds of letters, tables, hymns, songs, poems and the Lord's Prayer and we never questioned any of it. The playground shrieks would be tempered with, 'You're a better man than I am, Gunga Din!' How much we understood of Kipling, Jerusalem or Shakespearean songs I cannot tell, but the subjects came alive in the teaching so the learning was easy.

We were taught joined-up writing on creamy, smooth, pre-war paper, of which there were stacks still squirreled away in huge wooden cupboards. After mastering joined-up writing we were promoted from pencils to pens. Our inkwells were filled; we were each issued with a wooden-handled pen, a bright new nib and a piece of blotting paper (thereafter one piece per term and no more). Biros were strictly forbidden.

Miss Peacock was hot on spelling, so we did not dare be bad at it. Every evening we were set three words to learn for the next day. They were rarely less than three syllables and often floral in nature – chrysanthemum, nasturtium, antirrhinum, I particularly recall.

Games meant rounders in the stony playing field, on a slope, everything in Gloucestershire happens on a slope. We used old tin wartime ARP helmets for bases, which made a satisfying clang when struck with a rounders bat. The steep downhill run to first base, riddled with loose stones, was a test of the pupils' ability to stay vertical at speed.

The nearest thing we got to science was nature study. Sometimes this meant learning about the internal structure of the primrose, growing peas and beans in jars to see the roots, or fishing for caddis fly larvae in the old canal. Other times we would pillage the tangled valleys for specimens for the nature table. History was piecemeal and all I can remember is developing a passion for the Romans.

Girls who did well in any piece of work were sent to Miss Peacock by their teacher, clutching their efforts for her to scrutinise. There would be a few pupils every day, at lunchtime, lined up at her desk in a sort of quaking pride. After examining the work and approving it, Miss Peacock would sign it in green ink – the highest possible praise!

In spite (or because) of her eccentricities, our standards were generally high, though we all pitched in together, high-fliers and dullards alike. Parents from outside the catchment area pleaded to be allowed to send their daughters to Fanny Peacock. There was no question that 'her girls' would do well. She had probably never heard of feminism, but she made us want to work hard at whatever we did, developing as individuals before succumbing to domesticity. Whatever else we were, she wanted us literate and articulate. Everything was coordinated to get us ready for the 11-plus, just under half the class passing to the High School or the Girls' Tech. But Miss Peacock had time for us all, no matter where we went, and after Castle Street nothing was ever quite the same. We weren't just entering different schools, but a different era.

Pam Spokes, born 1949

Thrupp County Primary

I went to Thrupp County Primary School between 1948 and 1954 – a nice school with over 100 pupils. It was a good community school, drawing pupils from Thrupp and parts of Brimscombe. I remember school nature walks featured very strongly. We would go out through the gate and up into Thrupp woods. We learned a lot about wildlife – the names of flowers and birds. Children today seem to know the names of very few of these.

When I was in the Infants' Department at Thrupp School, after lunch you had your play and, when you came back in for the afternoon session, little folding beds were produced. The idea was that, in order to face the rigours of afternoon school, you were supposed to have a snooze for half an hour. Of course, most of us didn't sleep; we played games peeping at each other from under the blankets! Looking back, I suspect that this practice was intended for the benefit of the teacher as much as the pupils.

Howard Beard, born 1943

'Little Jim Fern'

My grandfather lived in Brimpsfield and he married my grandmother who lived in Miserden, hence we are really 'Stroudies', in the true sense. They were married in the 1850s and my grandfather was one of the first to move into Slad. The church was built in 1834, which was when it became a village. Four years later the school was built and all my father's brothers and sisters went to Slad School, as we children did too, in our turn.

Laurie Lee took me to school when I was three and he was a big boy of seven. We started in the Infants with hard slates and hard pieces of chalk, which screeched when you wrote on it. We also had the abacus, which was a good way to learn to count. In those days, the teachers knew the parents and the parents knew the teachers and, in my case, the whole family had preceded me. When you were five, you went into the main room of the school, which was a mixture of boys and girls, young and old. This is where I would have been when Laurie wrote the words, 'The Little Jim Fern, sitting beside me, looks up from his ruined pages. 'Ain't you a good scholar! You and your Jack. I wish I was a good scholar like thee', in his book *Cider with Rosie*.

We started with prayers then we chanted our mathematical tables, then we practised joined-up writing with sealed nib pens and inkwells and blots and then we used to have a bit of dictation. It was quite a good school. All children left at fourteen, unless they were fortunate enough to go a second school, but there were very few, as schools like Marling were fee-paying at the time and there were only a few free scholarships, provided by the wealthy industrialists. It so happened that Jack Lee, the eldest of the three Lee brothers, managed to pass for the Marling School. Laurie went to the Central School and this created a bit of jealousy right through their lives.

I was reasonably good and it was suggested that I would find it easier to get a scholarship if I came down to Uplands School, when I was nine. I passed to the Marling School and by the time I got there Jack Lee had become a prefect and there I was, 'Little Jim' sort of thing! Actually it was all right. It was a church school and you invariably got a visit from the vicar and the old squire in the mornings.

In the last year, one day a week the girls would go down to the British School to learn domesticity and boys would go to Brick Row to do carpentry. You stayed at Marling to sixteen but thereafter you started looking around for local jobs, as there was very rarely the money to carry on schooling.

Jim Fern, born 1918

Rodborough Secondary Modern

I went from Parliament Street to Rodborough Secondary Modern; my younger brothers went to up to the Manor School at Eastcombe. We used to have to walk home to dinner, all the way to Summer Street! We'd start off and, inevitably, we'd be distracted by something on the way; no sooner we'd be home, than it would be time to get back to school. Because we were such a big family, we were entitled to free school meals but it wasn't a very nice thing to carry with you, really, so we didn't have them.

At the bottom of Rodborough Hill there used to be a bakery, in what is now the art shop. In the winter we always used to get a roll to go up the hill: the fellow would pull them out on a tray and they would be steaming; they were a penny. I have really fond memories of that bakery and the smell!

My last term at Rodborough School was the first term that Archway opened. I left at fifteen and started work at Holloway's Clothing Factory.

Geoff Franklin, born 1946

Ebley School and then to Marling

I was born in 1926 in Ebley. I went to Ebley School in Chapel Lane at the age of four. Boss Nash was the headmaster and I always thought what an enormous man he was, but in my twenties I went back and realised that he was actually quite small. At the time there was the Ebley Orphanage at Ebley House, which was all girls and they were all marched up to school every morning for the nine o'clock chapel service.

At the age of eleven I went to Marling School. Marling was an excellent school – very small, only about 200 boys. It was an old-style school; there was no way you could go in without a cap and tie and in the summer you were expected to save up and buy a blazer; it cost £300 per year in those days.

It was a soccer school at that time and I remember playing for the junior side as an outside left against Cirencester Grammar School. Nick Carter was our headmaster and in January 1938, he decided to try rugby football to see how it went. We were lucky to have Mr H. Waldron, a teacher who became an international rugby referee, and Mr Oliver Wicks, who was second master and who had played rugby for Bristol University and Cinderford. We also had a number of masters who had been to Rugby School and were able to help out. So that's how Marling became a rugby school.

John V. Smith, born 1926

Cap, blazer and short trousers

I had a pushbike, which was bought for me from Curry's in Stroud for £2 6s, as my prize for passing to the Marling School in 1936. My auntie and granny lived in London Road and the day I passed I had orders to go down and see them in my cap, blazer and short trousers, so they could see what I would look like when I was going to school. Marling was in the main building, much as it is now, and you had the sixth form in a room to the left of the main entrance. Marling had not amalgamated with the Craft School at that point. The High School was very separate; there was no link at all. The headmaster was Mr H.W. Carter and the deputy was Mr W.O. Wicks (he taught

Latin, but he gave up on me!). The English teacher was Mr Jimmy Nicklin.

Dennis Mason, born 1925

Marling memories

In 1954, I went to Marling School. I remember my interview with the headmaster, Mr Annett, who read a short passage from the Old Testament to me, including references to something called Behemoth. He asked me what I thought Behemoth was (it's a huge or monstrous creature). I had no idea and was consequently convinced that I had failed to get in, although I had already passed the written part of the exam. The question obviously wasn't that important.

Everybody was supposed to enjoy milk in those days and at Marling the teacher who taught the lesson before morning break would make a tally of the required number of small bottles of milk and send off a monitor to fetch them.

I recall the dining hall at Marling. Once, when we were in it, a spider descended from the ceiling. I was offered a bet to eat this spider and I decided I would take it up for the sixpence on offer. I put the spider on to a small piece of lettuce, wrapped it up and ate it. I got my sixpence! School meals were cooked on the premises, but I think some people brought their own food.

When I was sixteen I started going out with a High School girl who was later to become my wife. We used to walk to school and back hand-in-hand. In those days some staff didn't consider this the right thing to do and we were both taken in front of our respective headteachers and told not to do it because it set a very poor example to the third forms! Sylvia and I both had arrangements set up whereby we could arrive in morning prayers a little late without being noticed, so that we could have a few more minutes together. She had a friend who would bring her hymn book ready for when she joined the line leading into prayers. For me it was easier because the school choir sat in the gallery, at the back of Marling School hall. So, even if the service had already begun, I could hurry up the back stairs and join in the second verse of the hymn without anyone noticing.

Marling School put on many concerts. I remember one in particular: we were performing Haydn's *The Creation*. The opening part of that work is called 'A Representation of Chaos'. Mr Watson, the music master, raised his baton ready to start and brought it down. What happened was much more a representation of chaos than he expected, because half of the orchestra was playing *The Creation* and the other half was playing the National Anthem! I also remember the joint concerts we had with the High School. There was little contact with girls at sixth-form level, apart from these events, so we boys very much looked forward to them.

Howard Beard, born 1943

Miss Boreham's first appointment

I was Cecily Boreham's first appointment in November 1964. I came from Dursley, where I was teaching in a comprehensive school, to teach modern maths at the High School. I stayed until December 1989.

Howard Beard aged eighteen.

I arrived just as the High School was amalgamating with the Girls' Technical School under the headship of Miss Boreham. The girls wore pink and white shirts and grey skirts, a blazer and a deep pink tie. They wore black felt hats in the Junior School and straw boaters, which were very quickly abolished. The staff moved between the senior and junior schools on separate sides of Beards Lane; too much time was wasted if the girls had to move!

Prior to amalgamation, the ethos at the High School had been to work hard and attain good results, whereas in the Technical School the girls were prepared for local employment and followed either a craft or commercial curriculum. With amalgamation there was a new academic thrust, which didn't always go down well, and although many staff had already decided to go, some stayed: Mrs Ivy Clark; Joyce Grey, who became Head of Junior School; Pam Gorge, who taught History, and Zita Gisborne, who taught needlework. There was quite a marked difference between the two staffrooms, senior and junior, in the early days, but as time went on everything became more integrated. Pam Gorge was in the junior school for many years. She had her very own teaching style, was extremely kind and interesting and everybody remembers her. I think she must have been a revelation at amalgamation for the High School girls!

In the senior school the caretaker and secretaries were marvellous. John Davies would do absolutely anything for you; his father had been caretaker before him. Wenda Dainty, an old girl herself, was school secretary and was very supportive.

Miss Boreham was very able and the great thing was that she knew everybody – she learnt the names of the girls and their parents very quickly. She was a disciplinarian; she had high standards and you had to live up to them.

From the moment I joined in 1964 there was talk of reorganisation. Cecily had been told that, within a year or two, Stroud Girls' High School would become a comprehensive. It never happened. Thank goodness for the parents, because you can't fight the local authorities for years on end without thinking 'why bother?' But there were always new sets of parents and they were enthusiastic to keep the school as it was, which kept the momentum going. For the first two or three threats of reorganisation we had to drum up support from parents and elsewhere and it was exhausting. We were cut off financially and had no money to do anything. Archway and the other comprehensives received huge sums while our buildings deteriorated; they weren't great in the first place. We would even have to paint our own classrooms. The school was eventually awarded grant-maintained status in September 1990.

I remember feeling apprehensive about teaching in an all-girls' school, but once I was there, and the reason I stayed for so long, was that I realised the value of single-sex education, particularly in maths and the sciences, where traditionally girls had been squeezed out. Study at the High School has always had a focused edge and the girls there have proved that they are just as capable as boys.

Peggy Fowler

A civilised way to make a living

From the time we came to Stroud in January 1959 from Wellingborough, we felt settled here. The atmosphere immediately impressed me, the feel of the place. I was appointed Head of French at Marling. There was a good standard of entry, academically, among the boys and we had some very talented old boys: for example, Peter Hennessy, now Professor of Modern History at Queen Mary College, London, and Michael Angus, head of the

This shows the Lansdown School of Art, which in 1904 housed the first school for girls in Stroud. It moved to its current premises in Beards Lane in 1911 and is now the Stroud Girls' High School. (Photograph courtesy of Howard Beard)

Confederation of British Industry, to name but two.

At that time the boys were very well turned out and so were the girls at the High School. There was a marked difference in atmosphere between the two schools too. There was the 'Iron Curtain', a fence between the two schools, keeping the boys and the girls apart!

I came to a school where many of the staff had known no other school – there was a sense of stability about the place and a confidence between parents and staff which was a very rare feature (of course the down side of this was the tendency for things to become pickled!)

At that time in the Marling School staff-room there were certain people who sat in certain chairs and it was divided between the chess players and the bridge players! Staff would play during breaks, during lunch, and after school.

In 1965 Marling amalgamated with the Stroud Technical School for Boys, which had been where the junior school is now. Stroud High School had already amalgamated with the Girls' Technical School the year before and Miss Cecily Boreham had been appointed as Head of the two schools in 1964. After amalgamation at Marling, Mr Godfrey Jones insisted on merging the two staffrooms. The quiet chess and bridge playing was totally transformed; there were suddenly a lot of youngsters recruited, and they were noisy! It was a funny sort of staffroom, but it worked quite well. Some of the old Boys' Tech staff used to get together, but they were still happy to come into the main staffroom. The only real hiccup I remember was the fifth year pupils from the Boys' Tech coming into the Marling fifth year. They were a handful! There was a lot of change in our time, but it settled

To celebrate the centenary of the school, this photograph appeared in the *Stroud News and Journal* on Thursday 3 December 1987, under the headline 'Marling Spell it Out'.

down under Mr Godfrey Jones. It was a great time for Marling. There were many boys going up to Oxford and Cambridge on scholarships. It was a little country grammar school but the standards were extremely high, both academically and on the rugby field. There were fewer than 400 pupils when I arrived; after amalgamation the numbers grew to over 700. And the sixth form expanded too.

I became Deputy Head from 1978 to 1985, taking over from Oliver Wicks, and then I was Head for three years when the school was threatened with closure. While I was Head we celebrated the centenary of the school, and at the same time we were scheduled to close – they were going to close both Marling and the High School and make all schools in Gloucestershire comprehensives.

The school was eventually saved from closure and the Governors decided to apply for grant-maintained status. I was asked to stay on, but said no.

For me the job was about having contact with the boys and with my colleagues, not sitting behind a desk. It was a most civilised way to make a living and there were the holidays, which my wife and I both enjoyed. We had a jolly good life altogether and I finished as a headmaster on a headmaster's salary too!

After I retired and had left the school, boys I had taught who met me in the street would adjust their ties and tuck their shirts in! I would say, 'No, I've left, you don't have to do that any more!'

Michael Gray

Michael Gray with four of the members of staff to whom Professor Peter Hennessy dedicated his book *Never Again*, at the Reform Club in 1992. From left to right: Michael Gray, Peter Young, Peter Hennessy, Eric Pankhurst, Cyril Campbell.

Marling School Centenary Dinner, 1987. From left to right: Sir Charles Marling with former headmasters Michael Gray (1985-88), David Phillips (1971-85), L.E. Godfrey Jones (1959-71) and David Annett (1954-59).

four
Wartime

We were all at war

Then the dreaded day came and we were all at war. I was thirteen and a half and things began to change: blackouts, ration books, no more street lights, air-raid warnings, Home Guard, gas masks in cardboard boxes, and the men began to leave for war service. There was a feeling of uncertainty.

Reg Hancock, born 1925

Working at Gloster Aircraft Company

In 1936, I thought I would go to Gloster Aircraft Company to see if I could get a job. I was taken on as a clerk in one of the big workshops. It was a job to get there, you had to get there as best you could; there were very few cars and we were too far out at Brockworth for the railway. Later on, as the war developed, they put on the Bristol Blue Bus, which took everybody to work from different areas; they used to try and race each other over the top. I had to cycle from Slad, throw my bike in the George Tap – down below were the wooden garages or outbuild-ings where they kept the horse-drawn hearses – I used to chuck my bike in alongside the hearses and go out to the corner of King Street to run for the bus. If I missed it, I used to cycle at great speed all the way to Brockworth, through Painswick. Often, I used to be just going down Green Lane when they were sounding the first hooter and I would get there just in time to clock in. If you didn't clock in on time, they would dock your pay – and of course we weren't very highly paid. When I was twenty-one I got an extra tuppence an hour, so that was about one pound and tuppence I got.

The Gloster Aircraft Company was a huge place, with many hangars. At that time they were quite short of work; they were making the Gladiator, one here, one there. Then of course 1938 came, war was coming; everybody knew it was coming. Hitler was ranting away on the radio every night and the company started getting orders for 100 Gladiators for the Fleet Air Arm. Factory numbers built up enormously and precautions were taken for the expected war, including camouflaging all buildings. Gloster Aircraft was painted green and brown so that the buildings could not be seen by aircraft. I was working there on the Sunday morning war was declared. I remember being up in the canteen; you had to work Sundays and a couple of nights a week, there was no choice.

Test pilots flew across the fields; at lunchtime we used to go out on to the fields and one of the pilots would to be up in his Gladiator and come sweeping down across the airfield and everybody scattered.

Jim Fern, born 1918

Men and women worked together

In 1940 I started work: it was Sperry Gyroscope for me. Sperry's was an American company that made artificial horizons, directional gyros, anti-aircraft predictors; everything was for the war. Previously they used to do dyeing; it's Bonds Mill now, where they sell carpets. Hoffmann's was on the other side of the road behind the row of houses called Happy Land.

I was given no recognised apprenticeship but I did get one, just the same, and not just in engineering either, but also in life and living. You had men and women working together operating drills and lathes, capstans, milling machines, grinding machines and assembly, and seeing and listening was educational in all aspects! There was an attitude of, 'live for today, you don't know what tomorrow may bring'. Women became more liberated and more outspoken, more demanding and approachable.

I was paid threepence ha'penny an hour, to start. I was taught the fundamentals of all the machines and I learned how to operate them all in turn. I could read and use micrometers, Vernier's indicators, surface plates, V blocks, assembly and calibration. I was deferred until May 1945 when I was to report to Colchester Barracks. On 3 May, Hitler was dead and the war ended a few days later.

Reg Hancock, born 1925

The sky was red

I remember in the winter of 1940 standing outside with my mother and looking up over Rodborough Common; the sky was red where they were bombing Bath and Bristol. I remember vividly one night when they were bombing Coventry; there was a continual drone of German planes, they had such a distinct noise, they flew over and two hours later they flew back again. Coventry was flattened.

Dennis Mason, born 1925

Blasted tomatoes

There was one bomb dropped around here on Selsey Common and it blew some windows out of the cottages. Apparently the German planes did come up and attempt to bomb Hoffmann's or Sperry's – they followed the River Severn and then they followed the canal. There are thirteen bridges but they must have miscounted and dropped a lot of bombs into the fields. One of them hit Tudor's greenhouses at Eastington; he was a market gardener and the day after this happened he had a board up outside, 'Buy our blasted tomatoes for your chutney!' At one time people used to walk through those meadows looking for where the bombs had been dropped, and there were a few local characters who could remember exactly where.

David Russell, born 1939

Lights out

I was a firewatcher: I had a long black coat and an armband which said 'Firewatcher'. When the sirens went, you had to get up and go to this little hut, where the other firewatchers met. We all had torches and gas masks and tin helmets, and we had to go around making sure there were no lights showing. The German aircraft were going over to Bristol, but you never know, if they had seen a light on the way over they might have dropped a bomb on Stroud. If you went down my back path, you could see the bright light of the flames where they were bombing Bristol.

Dorothy Harding, born 1922

Digging

When I was at school in my last year, Form 4 – we were the big ones with the long trousers – we actually dug the air-raid shelters for the Central School. A builder came and marked it out on the sports field at the back of the school, quite near the Girls' High School, and we were out there for a good three weeks or more digging. When we'd dug this zigzag trench down to about four feet, carpenters came in and put up a wooden framework with corrugated iron on the top, we then spent another week out there covering over the corrugated iron with the stuff we'd dug up. It wouldn't stand a hit but it would save you from shrapnel.

Ron Grange

Will they ever come back?

I was fourteen when the war broke out. My brothers were all there, sat down in chairs, when it was declared. So was Harry Davies, from Ebley, who went through the war with my brother John Victor. The twins were at home for about a year and then they both went into the Navy without being called up.

Three of May Bell's brothers, Nutty, Ronald and Donald Curtis, with their mother and Vicky the dog before the war.

Mother cried, 'My boys are going. Will they ever come back?' I have often thought of my mother in the war days. How did she manage, thinking of her four boys? The twins had been working at Newman and Hender's, Jack worked at Redler's and Nutty was in the piano works at Woodchester, but within a matter of a year they were all gone.

May Bell Dullea, born 1925

A full day's work

My father worked at Hoffman's factory during the war and his job was making bullets. He was an inspector in the factory, but he was also a Special Constable and part of his duties was to go up onto the roof of Rodborough Fort at night to watch for incoming German aircraft, which must have been fairly exhausting after you'd done a full day's work elsewhere.

Howard Beard, born 1943

Sperry's

I worked at Sperry's from 1940. We were sent to war work and we had to go. Some were sent to Newman Hender's and some to Hoffmann's and some to Sperry's. I was on testing, measuring things, and then, after a while, I started doing all nights because we had a bus to Oakridge that I could go on. The factory was working twenty-four hours a day during the war.

Ena Smith

He got six months

During the war people worked very hard in the munitions factories: Hoffmann's, Daniels and Newman Hender's were all making things for the war effort. Workers at Hoffmann's and Sperry's were doing twelve-hour shifts. There was a well-known character called Hedley Harmer who worked at Sperry's on twelve-hour shifts. In 1942 we had a nice bit of weather and he took his family down to Brighton for a fortnight. Course, leaving your war work was a crime and when he came back he got six months in Gloucester jail!

David Russell, born 1939

War work at Daniels

Daniels carried on quite a bit of their normal production during the war – machines for moulding things, presses and injection moulders – that was just a matter of changing the tooling and you could still produce what you like on there – machines were still wanted. But we had an aircraft section that made parts for Bristol aircraft; the pumps that could pump the undercarriages down by hand, the hydraulic

The Subscription Rooms during the war years, when an air-raid shelter was built on the forecourt. (Courtesy of Peckham's, Stroud)

cylinders that could operate the flaps – we made all sorts of hydraulic stuff there. With Bristol being bombed in the '40s, aircraft production was dispersed across the region. At Daniels there was a whole building devoted to Parnell's, an aircraft company at Yate, which had been badly bombed. They had been making gun turrets for training.

In the plate shop, which dealt with sheet metal, they were making thousands of bomb cases. You could walk in there and see rows and rows of them. We rolled the cylinders and welded them, the nose cones got red hot and were blanked out on the press. They were drilled and tapped for where the fuse goes in, there were lugs welded on the side and they had to be tested – you don't want the bomb dropping off the hook when it's going up into the aircraft. That went on for several years. There were special orders too, some seven or eight feet long. Some said they were for chemical weapons, but we never really knew.

During the war years there were over 600 people working at Daniels – I knew because working in the tool room we used to keep a tools record of who had borrowed what in the factory. But the office side hadn't really built up at that time.

Ron Grange

Cannon in the skip

I heard that during the war period Daniels was used to help make weaponry of all descriptions. The company used to get a lot of wrought iron delivered to the foundry to be melted down. On one occasion, of all the items that happened to be in the skip, was a small cannon, which caught my grandfather's eye. It was removed and to this day it still stands outside the reception, on a little carriage!

Jonathan Daniels

Inside the Daniels News, *the Editor writes:*
'Did you know that the cannon outside the Daniels Front Office was a Russian one? Technically known as a carronade and originally cast in 1807, the cannon was mounted on the battlements of Sebastopol, then captured by victorious British troops in the Crimean War.

At the end of this war, three such cannons were presented to the Stroud Subscription Rooms. Then came the Second World War, and the three Russian cannons were taken away for scrap. For some reason or other, the cannon now outside our Works was never broken up and Mr H.B. Dauncey, then a Director of the Company, suggested that it should be bought and preserved. Expert advice was obtained on mounting the cannon – the elevating screw, ratchet and wheels were actually made at Lightpill. So there it stands – once Russian, and now part of the Daniels scene.'

No railings

I remember when they took the gates off all of those houses on the row called Happy Land, and they took everybody's railings as well. Most of the wrought iron went down to Newman Hender's and some to Daniels. If you go along Horns Road and up to the cemetery, there are no railings: they took them all away during the war and they never replaced them.

Reg Hancock, born 1925

German plane at Oakridge

One hot afternoon in June 1940, we'd had our lunch at about 2 p.m. when we suddenly heard a noise; we looked up in the sky and saw what looked like huge puffs of cotton wool. This was the famous occasion when the German plane was shot down at Oakridge, a Junkers 88. We all cheered, but sadly a British plane came down as well. In the evening I got my pushbike and I rode up there and I pinched, or rather 'obtained', a piece of the German plane, which I took home and stored up with some other war memorabilia I had. Dad was in the Home Guard during the war and they were all called out to Oakridge. One of the crew surrendered himself up to Charlie Weston; one was found hanging in the tree and was buried at Brimscombe, before being taken back to Germany.

One of the pilots definitely did give himself up, but to whom was always a bone of contention! During the war years, newspapers had to be very sketchy about what they

The cover of the Daniels magazine showing the cannon outside the office block.

reported. If there was a tribute to a certain person who claimed the German had surrendered to him, someone else would say 'Oh no, he surrendered to me!'

Fifty years later, at the *Stroud News and Journal*, we published something about the crash and a person wrote in to say we were wrong. And so it goes on. Everyone knows about the German plane at Oakridge.

Dennis Mason, born 1925

Chased into the shelter

When we started at Daniels, we were all given a card with the number of which air-raid shelter we were to go to. I always remember I was given No. 2, which was built into the bank by the lower entrance to Daniels. The first time we used them was in daylight, when a plane got shot down at Oakridge, a Junkers 88. The sirens went and we all went rushing out, and you could see gunfire and the plane going over – people were just stood around. Course, they had a Home Guard platoon at Daniels, and Charlie Wagstaff, who was like a maintenance foreman, was the sergeant in charge, and he came out yelling and chasing everybody into the shelter! Anyway that plane got brought down, and crashed in Strawberry Banks. I have still got a small piece of the plane somewhere: we had boys at the factory who came from Oakridge and they were flogging bits of it for souvenirs!

Ron Grange

Fantastic community spirit

There were three British restaurants in Stroud: one down in Bath Street, one in Bedford Street in the schoolroom and one in the Sub Rooms. You could go in there and get a meal in the daytime at a reasonable price. There was a fantastic community spirit.

Dennis Mason, born 1925

Queuing for food

Grandmother would send me into Stroud as a small boy when things became available. She would get news that International had some 'off the ration' cheese, so I went and got in the queue for it. It was orange Dutch processed cheese, and I remember the assistant was quite concerned that I wasn't with anyone else and I wasn't getting a second lot. I had a pound of this 'off the ration' cheese and brought it home and thought it was wonderful. Another time one of the shops had some tinned pineapple come in, that was a real luxury and I remember it was one tin per person. It wasn't uncommon to queue for things.

David Russell, born 1939

The Maypole

We never starved; we had all the shops. One was the Maypole shop in the High Street, which sold cheese and butter. I remember going shopping with mother and we used to go to the Co-op, which was in Chapel Street in those days, and then we would go into the Maypole and mother would order a pound of butter. I would stand in amazement watching the man with two wooden pats throwing the butter up in the air and catching it; he never dropped it. There were lots of little stores during the war. Stroud was a thriving town until the '60s, when the environment changed completely.

Dennis Mason, born 1925

Fighting on a Friday night

The workhouse closed and during the war the Americans used it as a barracks; there were hundreds of them in there. There were also some at Lypiatt. Quite a number of the girls fell for the Yanks, who supplied cigarettes, silk stockings, drink and, in some cases, unwanted presents. Fighting was a regular thing on Friday and Saturday nights between the various units stationed at Edge and Aston Down. The ladies were mostly the cause; that and the amount of money the Americans had in comparison with our forces; the Yanks were loaded! Our men couldn't compete and that's why there were so many fights.

Reg Hancock, born 1925

Survived in the woods

Two of my brothers were prisoners of war: Jack was taken to Poland and worked in a mine and Nutty went into the Grenadier Guards and went to the desert. We heard from Nutty several times, then suddenly nothing. We had a wire from the War Office to say he had been taken prisoner, believed dead. They didn't send belongings back or anything. Eighteen months went by and my father would say, 'He won't die, he won't give in', and he was right. At last the postman came with a letter from Nutty. He had escaped off a train when he was being taken to somewhere in Italy. He lived for eighteen months in the woods on birds and berries and a little girl used to take him food. When he came back home, he was asked to go up to the Ritz cinema in Stroud and go

Reg Hancock in 2004. (Photograph by Peta Bunbury)

on the stage for people to ask him questions about his experiences. It was terrible when I saw him though; he had lost so much weight and he had gone completely grey.

May Bell Dullea, born 1925

Dive under your bed

At first, I went to work for the Air Ministry, which had moved their accounts departments down to Stroud from London. Then I joined the Royal Corps of Signals but I didn't go out of the country. I joined in 1943 and a year later they were getting ready for D-Day. I was in Richmond in Surrey when I went down with pleurisy. I went into Richmond Hospital and they discharged me from the services as medically unfit. My memories of the war were lying in a hospital bed. I remember vividly 6 June, we heard a noise and we looked up and there were hundreds and hundreds of aeroplanes going over to Normandy. About a fortnight later we heard a strange noise and it was the doodlebugs coming over and the orders from the nurses were to stay in bed as long as you can hear the engines going, then when the engine stops, get out and dive under your bed.

Dennis Mason, born 1925

Preparing for a catastrophe

When war was imminent, exercises were carried out, so that if some catastrophe occurred people would be prepared: places set aside to take the injured, and so on. I was with the Red Cross and I would play the part of a casualty, and the medical attendants would have to come and find me.

Jim Fern, born 1918

Stroud Entertainments Committee

During the war years there was a Stroud Entertainments Committee, and they ran concerts to raise money to provide cigarettes and things for the troops. They also held Sunday concerts alternately at the the Gaumont and the Ritz. They had the top stars, like the Squadronaires; you name them, they all came to Stroud.

Dennis Mason, born 1925

Evacuated to Stroud

I was evacuated to Stroud when I was sixteen, as a schoolboy at Handsworth Grammar School in Birmingham. The bulk of boys from my school had been evacuated by train in September 1939, but I went by coach in October because my parents couldn't agree on my future: my father wanted me to leave school and get a job but my mother wanted me to continue with my education. She won the day.

My first billet was with a Mr and Mrs Wheatley who were caretakers for a school in the town centre. I joined my close friend Herbert (Syd) Sharpley who was already there and we were made very welcome, in fact the Wheatleys could not have been kinder.

The Birmingham contingent were schooled at the Marling School; one week we would go to school in the morning and the Stroud children would go in the afternoon, the following week we would swap over and so on. This was a new arrangement and was experimental for everyone, but I think most would agree that it was a success.

We didn't have that much contact with local people other than our hosts and their families. Mr and Mrs Wheatley had a married son called Frank who was factory manager at Erinoid at that time. He took us to the factory and showed us round once. He was a nice chap; he lived in Thrupp with his young wife Amy, who used to tease us, I remember.

Syd and I stayed with the Wheatleys until mid-February 1940. That was a severe winter

Above: Eric with Mr and Mrs Wheatley. *Below*: Northfield House, Folly Lane, Stroud,

and poor Mr Wheatley became very ill and took to his bed. We would have stayed with them but for his health. There was a Mrs Angel in charge of new billets and she found us a place at Stafford House, the home of a retired Captain Robertson and his wife. I remember going there the first day and Mrs Robertson opening the door to us and saying, 'Oh, you can't come today; the Captain's a little seedy'. That has always stuck in my mind!

They were a rather grand couple and we had to mind our Ps and Qs. They had an orchard and the Captain kept fowl; they had no tablecloths, only lace mats, and the furniture was highly polished, which made a big impression on a boy from a working-class background. The Captain drank whisky and wasn't very friendly, although we ate well and on cold winter nights Mrs Robertson would wrap hot bricks in flannel and put them in our beds. We left after a fortnight because the extra workload was affecting her health.

Our third billet in Stroud was at Northfield House in Folly Lane, the Uplands. Syd and I were part of an advance party of fourteen boys – the numbers eventually grew to forty, all under the supervision of Mr 'Baggy' Lindon, a senior French master and his wife. The food was poor at Northfield: breakfast was porridge and bread and jam, and it was bread and jam for tea; at dinnertime, we would go to eat at one of the British Restaurants set up in Stroud, but although we had enough to eat, there was very little variety. Mum would send me food parcels from time to time, with biscuits and little squares of solidified jelly. I was always glad to get home and tuck into eggs and bacon.

Syd and I had a grand time as evacuees, with plenty of time to wander around, to swim and play tennis at Stratford Park. We went to the pictures quite regularly too; the Ritz and the Gaumont. The months in Stroud

Mr 'Baggy Lindon' and his wife.

formed the most carefree period of my life. I was always delighted to walk and ride in the countryside and we went as far as Cirencester and Gloucester and I loved the Slad Valley and Cranham Woods. Since then, and because of the happy memories, my wife and I have returned to Stroud for our holidays, staying at the Bear at Rodborough.

Eric Armstrong

Ebley Mill

In the late 1930s, Stanley Mill and Ebley Mill were working on a whole range of fabrics: men's suiting and ladies' costuming in a variety of colours and designs. As the war became more obviously imminent, the manufacturing changed over to a portion of military production, weaving Angola shirts, which were a mixture of nylon, cotton and wool, into khaki shirting.

A great friend of mine, Norman Hiscocks, and I decided to enlist, despite being given reserved occupations at the mill. I went into the Air Force and he in the Army and we both did our six years. The mill then moved from Stanley Mill, which was requisitioned by the Admiralty as a store, and it moved all its processing to Ebley Mill, which worked as a vertical processing mill again for the first time. After the war, Arthur Winterbotham offered me my job back as well as a couple of mill cottages to live in with my new family. It was an altered mill I came back to, and I had to renew all my studies in Stroud Tech.

Jack Marshall

Variety concerts and dance halls

They used to have concerts at the Ritz every Sunday night during the war; variety concerts, with all the well-known people of that time, mostly from London. I went every Sunday, except one, when we had an icy day in 1940. And on Saturday nights every village hall would have a dance. Sometimes the barracks had dance halls and they would send in a ten-tonner to pick up the girls from Stroud and take them back home again.

Dorothy Harding, born 1922

Ready for invasion

The Stroud Home Guard started as the LDV, or Local Defence Volunteers. They used to train on Sunday mornings. It's not quite as the BBC depicts in their *Dad's Army* programme but there was quite a lot of truth in some of that! There were various vantage points at which you would have to tackle the Germans: one of them was at the junction of Bisley Old Road and Bisley Road. Also down at Bowbridge: even now, if you go down to the traffic lights where it says Bowbridge Lane, you will see a metal hook in the wall. If the Germans came down Butterow Hill, the Home Guard was going to put a steel hose across to stop them. Up until 1940 the war didn't mean much, but when we suddenly realised that they were only twenty-two miles away on the other side of the Channel, it became a reality. We really began to think. We dug an air-raid shelter in our back garden. Everything was so orderly in those days.

Dennis Mason, born 1925

Celebrating VE Day

I remember VE Day: we went to Stroud with our little flags and we caught the five past two bus driven by Mr Sammy Adams. When we got to the Stroud Brewery and the railway bridge, the bus couldn't go round to the station yard because of the huge crowds and we had to get off the bus at the bottom of Rowcroft and walk up into the town with all the dancing going on in the streets. It was very exciting but poor Mr Sammy Adams was most distressed because he couldn't take the bus to its full journey – in those days, the older workers did everything on time and for the bus to be late and not even get round to the station yard, the poor bloke didn't know what he was going to do.

The police were in the centre of Stroud and they diverted one of the buses from Lewis and Godfrey's past Lloyds Bank down to Merrywalks but of course the bus would only just go down Rowcroft Retreat with an inch to spare either side.

David Russell, born 1939

five

Industries

T. H. & J. DANIELS, LTD., STROUD
HANDBOOK

Front cover of the Daniels handbook of 1948, showing the main works at Lightpill.

T.H. & J.D. Daniels Ltd, Stroud

Held in great esteem

I joined Daniels on the administrative side in 1946. Daniels was then a family firm, held in great esteem and properly recognised as caring in every facet of local life: social welfare, religious activities, scouting, council work and education.

It is said that in 1840 two brothers, Thomas Henry and Joseph Daniels, were walking up the rough, stony road from Lightpill when Joseph threw a horseshoe over the hedge, where the present entrance is situated. They decided that would be the site to build their blacksmith's shop and forge.

Daniels' early business consisted of smithing, forging and general ironwork. The business expanded and in 1904 became a limited company. The development of gas plants and high-speed pumps began, supplied to local industries and mines, and the iron and brass foundry, which had been set up in 1870, was supplying castings used in the manufacture of Daniels products.

Jim Fern, born 1918

A family firm

Originally, the Daniels business built up in response to agricultural engineering requirements. We understand the original members of the family, who were blacksmiths, lived in Nympsfield and came from there to Lightpill. The business grew and they did a lot of machine repair work for Dunkirk Mills, which we know from some old correspondence. From there, they made gas engines and were very well known for making presses: apparently you didn't look too far if you needed a press, you went to Daniels for it. Daniels ran apprenticeships and trained their newcomers in 'The Art of Moulding', presumably to make

Thomas Daniels, founder of the firm.

the metal take different forms and shapes. They took a lot of apprentices on, everyone had to sign the indentures but it was a very popular and well-respected apprenticeship.

Juliana Daniels

Five-year apprenticeship

I left school in 1939, at the age of fourteen, and I went straight to Daniels. I think there must have been at least six or seven of us that went then. Mr Dauncey, who was the works manager there in those days, was always very keen to get pupils from the Central School because it was a craft school; I mean, we had workshops and we knew all about engineering. We were asked to come over for interview and we were all interviewed as a block and we all started work the same day. You get check numbers in factories and we all had consecutive numbers.

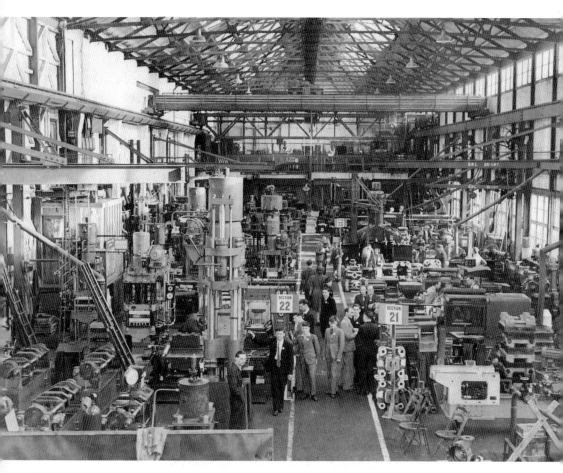

The works at Lightpill in the 1950s.

We used to say Daniels was the best place to do an apprenticeship. We went there on a year's probation and then we were signed up; my father came down and met Mr Fred one Saturday morning and we went in the office and signed the indentures. It tied me to a five-year apprenticeship. You moved around various departments and in the end I might have gone into one of the offices as a draughtsman, but the war was still on, getting near the end, and I managed to stay there and be deferred till I was twenty, when I went into the RAF. I came back in June 1948.

Ron Grange

Variety of products

After the Great War, production reverted to peacetime needs and there followed a rise in the variety of products, the most significant of these being the design and manufacture of presses for the growing plastics and rubber moulding industry. During the Second World War, Daniels' products were again set aside in favour of making tank parts, parts for Bailey bridges, shell casings, tripods for gun emplacements and aircraft components. They also manufactured the first chainsaws for the MOD.

Jim Fern, born 1918

Ron Grange in 2004. (Photograph by Peta Bunbury)

Over 600 employees

Post-war, there was new investment in machinery, but the company still maintained its forge, pattern shop, foundry and plating shop. There were two large machine shops housing planers, boring mills, grinding and drilling machines, lathes, capstans and tool stores. There was an electrical department, a maintenance department, a spares and service and repairs section – in other words, everything required for an engineering company. Other extensions were made including a new office block.

Up to this time, Mr Frederick and Mr John Daniels were the senior directors and Mr Fred's two sons, Lionel and Eric, were already playing a part in the further development of the company. It was Lionel, however, who took over the running of the firm on the death of his father in 1950, and who took the company forward. By the early '60s business was booming, there were over 600 employees, and training for staff and works at every level.

Jim Fern, born 1918

Post girl

I worked as an office junior at Daniels in 1948, and after nine months I got a job in the cost office.

It was useful there those first months; I learnt the telephone exchange and I got to know everybody that worked there because I was the post girl. Mr Percy Stanley was my boss. He was the buyer.

The overall director at the time was Mr Fred Daniels and one of my jobs was to collect the cheques and take them to him to sign. He used to deliberately miss one and see if I would pick it up – and if I did he gave me sixpence. Mr Fred had a great big American car and he used to pick us girls up sometimes and take us into Stroud at lunchtimes. He used to keep a clothes peg on the choke because it wouldn't stay out – it used to fascinate me, but why I remember that I don't know!

He was good to me was Mr Fred. When I was working at the Stroud Brewery a couple of people there had gone down with TB, and a couple of them died. I lost a lot of weight and I had to go for tests at the Stroud Hospital. Mr Fred thought I didn't look at all well and he thought it would do me good to have a holiday. He arranged it through Mrs Cullis, who was personnel, and I went to some friends of hers down at Weston-super-Mare for three weeks to convalesce, all expenses paid.

When I eventually got into the cost office they sent me down to Bristol for training as a comptometer operator (the forerunner of the computer really) and when I came back I had to put my expenses in. I said I had stopped with an aunt and he [Mr Fred] asked me if I had bought her anything. I said I had bought her a handbag; he wanted to know how much it had cost and he made sure he gave me the money for the handbag.

That was very much the essence of the company at that time – it was a family concern, they looked after you as if you were family. Mr Fred used to come in some days and he would bring his grandson, John, into the office and plonk him on my desk and say, 'Here Dora, look after him for me.' John must have been about six or seven and I was fifteen.

Dora Grange

Pioneers

Daniels used to do a lot of plastic injection moulding, one of which was the early flower-pots, which they pioneered, and the yoghurt cartons for Ski yoghurt. They made stone crushers and gas engines, which produced electricity. They were pioneers in that sort of work; there is still an early example of one such machine in Stroud Museum. They were exported to South America. They built a railway line in Bolivia, but you never have to go far to see the name Daniels in Stroud: it's on ironwork in some of the older buildings; on the attractive steel bridge at Stratford Park, on manhole covers, set into pavements, on canal bridges, such as the one down at Lodgemoor Mill, even at Stroud Station: the passenger footbridge has the name T.H. and J. stamped over it.

Jonathan Daniels

Dora Grange as a young lady, 1958.

Daniels workers demonstrate the chainsaw, 1948.

Hare-brain

Lionel was quite a hare-brain I think: he used to own a Jaguar and one day it caught fire and he was racing it to the fire station and people were trying to stop him. Anyway, he got there and asked them to put the fire out - mainly because he wanted to save the petrol!

Juliana Daniels

Great Uncle Eric

I do remember our Great Uncle Eric, Lionel's brother. He ran Daniels, Cam, which was a board mill. Eric lived in Stringers Court, a large house in Rodborough, and attached to it was Stringers Farm. He loved electronics and made small generators with Frankenstein-style wiring which made its way underground, through the cellars and back up into the house. In his enormous bedroom he had some see-through glass batteries; nowadays they would be thought of as very dangerous! He also liked fireworks and he used to make his own. I remember on one occasion sitting outside Stringers Court on a wooden bench, extremely close to some fireworks – possibly a bit too close. They were very noisy and bright; he'd probably added a few too many iron filings but they were extremely good fun!

Jonathan Daniels

Fred L. Daniels JP.

A big, extended family

In the heyday of Daniels there were 600 people working there, but in the '30s, when there was a great slump, my great-grandfather Fred would take his employees to work in his own home at Stringers Court, rather than lay them off. It was at that time they built a pond with a watercress bed and a lot of piping to drain the land and to re-route it down to the factory. He used to pay them out of his own pocket, but that was very much the style of the company, like a big, extended family.

The grounds of Daniels at Lightpill were very well kept, always a picture, with rose beds and dahlias. There were greenhouses and Mr Rodway one of the directors, even developed a delphinium. I remember rows and rows of dahlias as a child. There was a bank full of flowers behind Fern Cottage, which is where the Meningitis Trust building is now.

My grandfather, Lionel Daniels, was keen that the whole family should work together, and my mother used to say that often, if he and his brothers were digging the garden, they would dig it in a row, each one taking a row alongside each other. They were brought up to work together and that has continued; it works well for us.

Juliana Daniels

J. Lionel Daniels.

Never quite the same

Lionel Daniels was tragically killed in a car accident in 1958, after which the company was never quite the same again. The name T.H. & J. Daniels was dropped when Unichrome International took over. The company continued to trade profitably and new products were introduced. Consultants were brought in for restructuring, which inevitably led to redundancies, and the company, which had prided itself on its diversity, began to specialize more and more in the manufacture of moulding machinery. In the '70s the John Brown conglomerate acquired the company and there were more changes. It was now an American-owned business and it soon acquired an American MD, who moved to live locally, but, by now, the last vestiges of the Daniels family were gone forever, and I myself retired in 1982. The company went on trading in the reconstructed way until John Brown sold out to the Trafalgar Group; there was one further change of ownership, a Norwegian conglomerate named Kvaener, before closure in 1986.

Jim Fern, born 1918

Above and opposite: Open day at Daniels, 1948.

He didn't believe in seatbelts

Eric became chairman of the company for a while after Lionel died, but sadly he also died in a car accident. He didn't believe in seatbelts and was a passenger in a car at the Sapperton Tunnel crossroads. The car swerved, he fell out by some railings, but, to make matters worse, there was lorry behind which couldn't stop and he died more or less instantly. Both brothers were killed in their early fifties.

Jonathan Daniels

Kingpin

Lionel, my grandfather, had five children: my father John, Peter, Philip, Ruth and David. My father worked at Daniels but I was so young, I didn't really know what was going on when the business changed, after Lionel died. It is clear through and through that at the time my grandfather was very much the kingpin of the business, and if you wanted something to happen he made it work.

My father, John Daniels, also unfortunately died at the early age of fifty-two. I was close

to him and worked with him on our farm, which had many connections with the business. Daniels used to make a lot of water vessels and tanks, which needed testing; one way of testing them was to fill them up with water, but to acquire the water they captured a lot of natural springs on Stringers Farm, above the factory at Lightpill, and actually piped it to Daniels. The pipework still exists today and flows out into the River Frome. They needed a lot of water for testing and for the foundry. The piping is quite clever engineering. There

was a lot of water captured under Spillman's too and piped back to Lightpill in cast-iron pipes to a big tank under the factory. It crops up from time to time when various workmen start digging!

Jonathan Daniels

The hatchet men
Anybody who had worked at Daniels for twenty-five years was given a gold watch and became a member of the '25 Club'. I had mine

The '25 Club', April 1966. Ron Grange is in the front row, second from the left.

in 1965 – they kept me on the books even when I was away in the services – solid gold and engraved on the back with your name and T.H. and J. Daniels. We had a party too – mine was at the Manor School, Eastcombe (Thomas Keble now) and we all had to file up and go on the stage to be presented with our watches and a special tie.

When John Brown owned Daniels they had assessors come in, but we called them hatchet men. If we saw them on the premises we knew that in a week or two's time there would be someone redundant. I was made redundant the last but one lot, about 1985, then the whole place closed. I went to Grundy's, which had been Sperry's during the war. When the hatchet men first came in the late '70s, we had small children and we were still sitting up in bed worrying about it at 2.30 in the morning.

Ron Grange

A works outing…

Daniels started in 1840 and their centenary year was 1940, but the war was on. The first opportunity to celebrate it was in 1948 when they decided to give everyone a day's holiday and a day's outing. It was all laid on; we had special trains. I remember catching a train from Nailsworth through to Dudbridge and we all went down to Bristol; we had coaches out

Ron and Dora Grange in 2004. (Photograph by Peta Bunbury)

to Hotwells and we got on the *Bristol Queen* paddle steamer! We went all the way down to Ilfracombe and we went to three different restaurants. We were all given different tickets because there were so many of us, we all had a god meal and then we came back by paddle steamer and train.

Ron Grange

...and a romance

The very first time I saw Ron was when I had been at Daniels only a few weeks and I was supposed to be going to the British Fair at Birmingham, but I was being sent to Weston, so I was cancelling my trip in the same office he was booking his. The centenary celebration day was a few months later. Going down on the *Bristol Queen* in the morning I was very seasick. He was nearby in his long raincoat and he put it round me and looked after me. It was rolling a bit; it was 18 September 1948. I had a ticket for one restaurant and he had a ticket for another – we went with different people. But coming back we sat in the lounge and I was perfectly all right. I got off the train at Dudbridge and he got off at Nailsworth, but we'd arranged to go out the following weekend – we went up onto Haresfield Beacon and we walked over the top.

Dora Grange

Holloway and Hill Paul

Today, instead of cumbersome crudely-driven machines, capable only of plain sewing, there are Singer sewing machines of the very latest types for such diverse processes as Button-holing, Button-sewing, Basting, Seaming, etc.; with short benches and separate drives. Instead of bare rooms, with naked gas-jets and heated by stuffy stoves, there are great airy apartments, with large windows, electrically lit and automatically warmed and ventilated in both summer and winter.

The first Holloway workroom in Stroud has now grown into an imposing building of three stories, with a frontage over 100 yards, situated in Church Street, and the number of workpeople has increased steadily so that this flourishing Stroud industry now gives employment to over 750 workpeople.

The growth of this firm has been closely identified with the growth and progress of the town

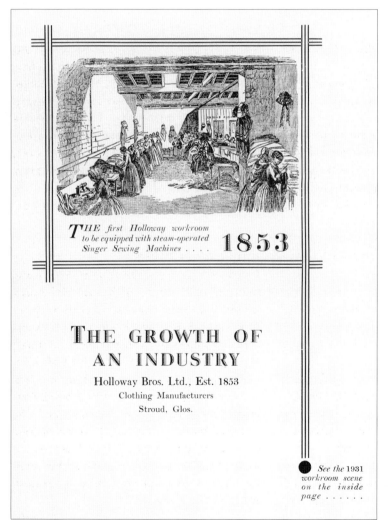

THE first Holloway workroom to be equipped with steam-operated Singer Sewing Machines **1853**

THE GROWTH OF AN INDUSTRY

Holloway Bros. Ltd., Est. 1853
Clothing Manufacturers
Stroud, Glos.

See the 1931 *workroom scene on the inside page . . . . . .*

The front cover of Holloway's promotional brochure, 1931.

STROUD, GLOS.

Telegrams:
HOLLOWAY'S, STROUD.
Telephone: 99.

London Office:
LEITH HOUSE, CORNER OF GRESHAM ST
& WOOD ST, LONDON, E.C.4.
TELEPHONES: CITY 0553 & 0554

Irish Office:
50, UPPER QUEEN ST,
BELFAST

Regency CLOTHING

TRADE   MARK

August 31st. 1931.
As September 20th.

M essrs. S. & S. Senior.
Baille Street.
ROCHDALE.

DR TO HOLLOWAY BROTHERS, LTD.

WHOLESALE & EXPORT CLOTHIERS.

Holloway's headed notepaper, 1931.

of Stroud, and Mr George Holloway in particular was one of Stroud's greatest benefactors. He was elected to represent the division in Parliament and sat for six years. His statue, which is a striking feature of one of the main thoroughfares of Stroud, attests the cordial recognition given to his ability and character. It is erected outside the Holloway Institute, and here it may be mentioned that Mr Holloway was founder of the Conservative Benefit Society, now called the Holloway Original Benefit Society, which has a membership of over 6,000, and was the forerunner of all the Holloway Societies in the Kingdom, the total membership of which is 209,000.

From the leaflet 'Growth of an Industry' produced by Holloway's in 1931

Ladies' work

Holloway's employed several hundred girls, mostly straight from school, some worked there for most of their lives; Hill Paul and Strachan's were the same; Ham Mills, Stanley Mills and Longford's, all cloth mills, also employed mostly ladies.

I remember the hooter at Holloway's blasting out at 1 p.m. for lunch and hundreds of girls would scatter in all directions for their dinner, up the pitch to Leazes or Summer Street, Bisley Old Road, Horns Road and Lower Street and back again by 2 p.m. This would happen again at 6 p.m. Salmon Springs, the bottling department for Stroud Brewery, also employed many ladies. The Stroud area was full of industry: Chalford and Nailsworth Valleys, Daniels, Waller's, Newman Hender's, the piano works and many more, and the town reflected it all.

Reg Hancock, born 1925

Forty-eight-hour week

I went to Oakridge School until 1935. I was fourteen and I went straight into Holloway's where I worked from 8 a.m. to 6 p.m., Monday to Friday, and 8 a.m. to 11 a.m. on Saturday mornings, which made it a forty-eight-hour week. I was living at Far Oakridge. Holloway's would pay your fare on the bus but not on the railcar and after a while, they bought me a bicycle and I used to cycle to and from work. At that time I was being paid six shillings and sixpence a week. I had to give some of my money to my mother. One sister went into service and my other sister worked at Daniels in the office.

Ena Smith

Holloway's workroom, 1931.

Hill Paul

I was the youngest of the family. My brother Robert was the oldest, then Dolly, Nora, Gladys and Edna, then one died, a girl, I never knew her name, and then me. I can remember Robert getting married; he was working at Daniels. I was the baby, as spoilt as you could get in them days. There wasn't a lot of money around but plenty of rabbits! I got a scholarship to go to the Central School from Whiteshill Boys' School, I was there to twelve, and then I went down to Central School. I met Laurie Lee at the Central School. We used to have violin lessons together. You were supposed to stay at the Central School until you were sixteen but in 1931, when I was fourteen, Father was out of work and I got a job at Hill Paul's: a forty-eight-hour week for ten shillings a week.

I was at Hill Paul's for twelve months and as a boy there I had a sort of dual job: I was in the warehouse in the afternoons and in the cutting room in the mornings, stamping the tickets for the garments as the orders came up. The measure cutters wrote their own tickets, they were the elite. I was a boy in knickers! The only pair of long trousers I had was a pair of overalls.

Ken Toomer

Affordable housing?

Holloway's put some red-brick houses up on Dorrington Terrace and two rows of red-brick houses in Horns Road. They were meant to be affordable housing, built for the workers to buy, but only one worker ever bought and that was a lady called Miss Munt. They were three

Holloway's clothing factory in Brick Row, *c.* 1910. (Photograph courtesy of Howard Beard)

shillings and threepence a week, bar the one that we lived in which was four shillings and a penny, because we had a shed on the side. Even in those days my grandfather, James Butt, couldn't buy himself a house. That would have been about 1880.

Ken Hill, born 1915

I used to like sewing

I used to like sewing. We went into the juvenile room while we were training, making 'knickers' as we called them then: short trousers. All the boys wore short trousers; they didn't all wear long trousers like they do now. Then I went into the trouser room, until I was sent to work at Sperry Gyroscope for war work, and then I had to go all the way to Stonehouse.

I got married and had two boys and I didn't go back to work until 1967, but Holloway's used to send me the work at home. They provided the machine and I still did trousers. You made them right the way through; not the button or buttonholes, though, that was done by machine. Then they brought in zip fly-fasteners and I had to go into the factory for a day to learn how to do those.

Ena Smith

Learn the trade

My dinner hour at Hill Paul was 12-1 p.m. and from 1-2 p.m. I was supposed to sweep the cutting room up and make it clean and tidy, but the cutters never wanted to leave the cutting room to let me get on and sweep up and of course the pipe-clay dust would rise. I learnt the job off an old chappie called Les Miller. They give him the sack because he was earning seventeen shillings and they could pay me ten. Poor old Les got killed in the war. They put him off after he taught me everything I knew, and I never seen him from that day to this. I was only a kid, I didn't realise what was going on.

I was not very happy in the cutting room so I left at fifteen. I got a job in the foundry at Daniels because my brother worked there doing fitting and turning. It was very hot and dirty in them days and one day I got burnt. When they were casting, when all the metal was liquid in the furnace, a chap named Nutty would hit a hole in the bottom and there was a big cradle underneath and I had to stand there with this long piece of iron; they would pour the metal into the mould and I would stand there and skim the muck off the top. One day the mould hadn't been lined and I got burnt. After that, I decided to go for a job at Holloway's. I thought I would settle down and learn the trade. I became a trimming boy.

Ken Toomer

It was magical

I left Rodborough School in 1961 at fifteen and started work at Holloway's clothing factory in general maintenance; there was a sewing machine mechanic and electrician, Clive Olpin, a general builder, Mark Smith, and a boiler man, Alan Basset, and I lent them all a hand. It was wonderful because they had a steam engine, which generated their own electricity and their own steam for the steam presses. There were two massive big boilers that you had to stoke with coal to get the engines going; it was magical! There were a lot of different departments: shirt, trousers, suits, the whole lot. A fellow called Mr Bendle was in charge when I was there. Adrian Holloway was there for my interview, which was quite intimidating.

Geoff Franklin, born 1946

Never looked back

Trade was unpredictable at Holloway's in the '30s; it would fluctuate. From Easter through to July you'd work from seven in the morning until seven at night, but then trade would drop off and they would only keep the big six cutters working a forty-eight-hour week. I went down to Arthur Woolley's in Stonehouse and learnt the art of producing patterns, but that didn't make you a 'special' cutter. When you were a measure cutter like me, you just had the basic pattern and you had to manipulate the patterns to fit the customer.

Bert Ingram was responsible for cutting all the ski-wear, school-wear and the fantastic array of stuff for the Cape (that's South Africa). When he died, a chap called Les Stockwell got the job, but then he was promoted to ladies' cutting and I fell into Bert's job. That job was busy from August to the next spring, but the foreman, a chap called Reg Austin, was artful – he would keep me in one week and put Les in the next, so we were still in and out of work all the time.

By now, though, I had learned enough; I could cut a pair of trousers without the pattern and I went back to Hill Paul and saw the gaffer, John Paul, and he said to me 'What can you do?' and I said, 'I can produce a pair of trousers and I can get by'. He said, 'When can you start?' and I said, 'Any time to suit you', and he said, 'Start next Monday'. So I did – I went back to Hill Paul's and I never looked back.

There used to be sixty-five people working in the cutting room at Holloway's in those days, but at Hill Paul there was just Bert Davies, Ray Phelps, Alan Browning, Darky Innes, Ken

Price, myself, Charlie Chamberlain, Geoffrey Higgins, Ted Clarke and Bert Bushell.

Hill Paul's had a different outlook towards their employees. Short-time working in the clothing trade was always a hazard, but I've known John Paul split an order up to spread it round the shop to keep people in work, when one man who could have done it.

Ken Toomer

A nice family set-up

In those days you were allowed the radio on twice a day at Holloway's: *Workers' Playtime*, *Family Favourites* and so on, and there was this one lady, Nancy someone, whose job it was to turn the radio on and off again. She used to live up Spider Lane. I was only there for two years but it seemed like a nice family set-up. I was aware of Hill Paul, the opposition; my brother worked there as a matter of fact, as a cutter. At five to eight in the morning I blew the hooter and at five o'clock at night I blew the hooter. You had to wind the wheel up really quick to get a clean sound, otherwise it would make a slow rising sound. Those were the days when if you weren't into work by eight you weren't coming in!

Geoff Franklin, born 1946

It was a skilled job

I got settled down at Hill Paul and got on very well. I had a lot of help from a chap named Ken Price. A fair few of these chaps had come back from the 1914-18 war, they'd only been kids when they went out there, mind, Ken Price and Adam Browning and Walt Bingham; they was all took prisoners down the salt mines. Anyway, Ken Price, he was a good friend to me: you had to learn how to get the suit out of a certain amount of cloth; it all had to come out of three yards to make the job economical. It was a skilled job, although I don't think it was ever really appreciated as such.

On the measurer's side of the business, you had a set of measures come through and a description of the size of the figure – long neck, round shoulders, humpbacked – and you could manipulate your patterns, when you were clever enough to make the job fit. Course, a lot of people would have a try-on; it would pay to have a try-on, though you paid a bit more. There was a range of patterns and the customer would go into a shop to be measured, chose their cloth and the order would be sent into the factory. The suit would be cut out, made and sent to the person who ordered it. I was extremely lucky; I ended up cutting all the britches and pants, I also used to cut the wide winged-jodhpurs.

Ken Toomer

John ran the factory

Holloway's was in a better class of trade than Hill Paul. Holloway's had more variety; they were into ladies' work where there was more money. But there was a good atmosphere at Hill Paul; there always seemed to be a personal relationship with the staff. There were three brothers. John Paul was the senior, he literally ran the place, and he dictated the job. Then there was Alan Paul, and the young gov'nor was Will Paul, who lived round at Randwick; he stuttered, but he was a grand chap really. Alan and Will were 'on the road', commercial travellers. John ran the factory; he ordered the cloth, dished the work out. You could tell what mood he was in: if he called you 'Toomer' you kept your mouth shut, if he called you 'Ken' you was all right. I ain't telling lies!

Ken Toomer

Previous page: The Staff of Hill Paul clothing factory, *c.* 1901. (Photograph courtesy of Brian Moss)

Ena Smith and colleagues in Holloway's workroom, in the early 1970s.

The good old days

Holloway's used to have a jazz band, but I wasn't in it because I was living too far away to go for practices. They used to win quite a few prizes and I remember them at Stroud Show. We used to have works trips to Weymouth and Porthcawl at the weekends or sometimes in the holidays. You used to have one week's holiday a year, but you weren't paid when you weren't at work. That was the good old days!

Ena Smith

The 'fancy room'

They had a ladies' department at Holloway's, the 'fancy room' they used to call it, where they made skirts and things. It was mostly

Holloway's jazz band, 1936. (Photograph courtesy of Sue Tunnicliffe, whose mother Edna Young is pictured far right)

women working there, although there were men on the presses and it was all men in the cutting room. Women did the linings and the fittings. They stopped the trouser line and we were all put into the coat room about two or three years before the company closed in 1975.

Ena Smith

The mill industry

A working life in the mill

I was born in Totnes, Devon eighty-five years ago. I was brought up on the Dartington Hall estate where the Elmhursts, American sociologists, had set up a utopian community.

I was destined to study poultry farming but I hated it and eventually, when I was fifteen, there was a vacancy in the textile department and I was interviewed and taken on by a man called Arthur Winterbotham. He was a man with a magnificent mind and was a member of the Winterbotham family of Hunt and Winterbotham of Strachan's. He came to Stroud to become a director of Marling and Evans. His aunt lived at Stonehouse Court. By this time, I had started in the textile mill at Dartington, where I trained as a handloom weaver, but it was a very small department and, what's more, the Elmhursts thought that modern progress was outstripping the abilities of the local workforce, so they decided to revert to seventeenth- and eighteenth-century practices. So the mill at Dartington had a Spinning Jenny, a small hand-carding set, vegetable dyeing, various milling and fulling on the old principles. I didn't see much of a future for myself there and asked Arthur Winterbotham if there was a vacancy for me at Stanley and Ebley Mills.

When I came to Stroud in 1938, I jumped straight into the twentieth century; it was a bit of a shock. I started as a management trainee at Stanley Mill and eventually, over the years, I worked through each of the departments at both Stanley and Ebley Mill. Marling and Evans was a vertically-integrated concern, which means that the raw material came in at one side and came out finished at the other. The whole of the processing from fibre to cloth was done in the two mills. Normally it would have been done at one mill and in previous years the two mills had worked as vertically-integrated mills in their own right, but when Marling and Evans amalgamated they had been divided up, one mill did the carding and the spinning, the converting of wool fibre into yarn, and the other mill did the dyeing, the finishing and the converting into cloth.

I spent forty-six years in the mill and only six years away during the war: a working lifetime. There was a wonderful atmosphere and although wages were very poor, the camaraderie and esprit de corps were fine. As a young person who had come up through every department, I was always 'Jack' to everybody in the mill and there was a good relationship between workers and management. The workers also spent their lives at the mill; sometimes generations of the same family had worked there.

By 1968 the mill was running into difficulties. There were several reasons for this: one was the advent of the denim cloth which gave the West of England flannel its death throes; people began to wear casual car coats as opposed to West of England suits. No one was ready to buy West of England cloth; people were becoming more casual. With women's costuming in the old days we would regularly take prizes at Vogue for our designs, but we were dyeing and spinning to meet last year's predictions and the following year the fashion designers would say, for example, 'Stripes are out, it's all plain colours!' That is a wasteful way of producing cloth. There was a massive surplus, which was all scrapped.

We saw this coming in 1949 and we had to look for an alternative. We had done some work for Nylon Spinners, nylon having come in during the war, and we were asked to reproduce cotton fabric with manmade fibres. It became a second string to our bow – I developed cloths for a whole range of purposes, which were not fashion-related: protective clothing, anti-static clothing, incorporating steel for radar reflection. I applied my textile knowledge to these new fabrics.

Even with this diversification, we were still running into difficulties. We should really have built another factory and whole new system, but we had no capital, so we had to make do and mend, processing the manmade fabrics on machines made for woollen manufacture.

I retired when I was sixty-four in 1984. Marling and Evans was taken over by London financiers and became Marling Industries. When Ebley Mill shut down in 1967 we offered it to the council, with all its machinery in, as a museum, but they turned it down. Another man bought it from us for a pittance, sat on the property for about a year then sold it for a lot of money. It became Stroud's Council Offices in the '80s. The sad memories of seeing it in its broken-down state were overcome by the sight of the conversion done so admirably by the council – despite the cost!

Jack Marshall, born 1920

A history of the mill industry

There used to be over 130 woollen mills in Gloucestershire. There are now only two: Strachan and Co. at Cam Mills and Lodgemore Mills, which are owned by an American firm called Milligan.

Historically, the surroundings made the siting of mills in this valley natural: an abundance of lush grazing meant that the Cotswold sheep had a valuable quality of

Stanley Mill. This is a view of the mill from the Kings Stanley side of the river. Original waterwheels were internal; water from the river and the reserve pond fell 15ft and ran under the mill in culverts some 16ft below ground. The whole edifice was constructed on this restrictive foundation. (Photograph courtesy of Jack Marshall)

wool which lent itself to felting and good processing; water power came from the River Frome and rich deposits of Fuller's earth, used for cleaning cloths, were plentiful. The finest teasels for raising the cloth were propagated at Wootton-under-Edge and Bristol was a flourishing port, through which cut fleeces were exported to the Lowlands from as early as the thirteenth and fourteenth centuries. The Flemish weavers were the most advanced in Europe and our wool had the quality they were looking for, until the mid-sixteenth century, when we began to manufacture our own cloth.

The mills signalled the early start of collective working or the beginning of the factory system as we know it today. Before that, weaving was a cottage industry, a family affair. The first record of a mill on the site of Stanley Mills is 1551: a grist mill owned by a man named Clotterbacke (immediately anglicised to Clutterbuck) almost certainly a Flemish refugee, fleeing from religious persecution in his own country. The mill would have ground corn into flour and milled the hand-woven cloths, spun and woven by the local cottagers. The independence of the cottage weavers, however, was gradually eroded, with the invention of the flying shuttle in 1773 and the Spinning Jenny, which could do the work of twenty or thirty spinners.

Stanley Mill as we know it today was built in 1813. It was unusual for this part of the world because it was built of brick and not of the local Cotswold stone. It is a classic example of a fireproof factory, a showpiece of its day: stone-flagged floors, hundreds of cast-iron pillars, an absence of exposed timbers and metal doors separating the main workrooms.

Jack Marshall in 2004.
(Photograph by Peta Bunbury)

The Marling family bought the mill in 1842 for £27,000. They worked hard but were not tyrannical: they improved work conditions, built local churches and provided funds for the Marling School in Stroud. In 1920, P.C. Evans, already based at Ebley Mill, bought a major share in Marling and Co. and amalgamated the two companies to become Marling and Evans. Sir Henry Marling organised the changeover but then left the mill and from then on, although the name was retained, the Marling family ceased to be a part of the company.

From sheep's back to finished product – how cloth is made

In my day, the wool was bought from Australia and South Africa. A merchant would come to the mill with samples and you would use your expertise to examine price, colour and felting potential. You developed this ability over a long period. The wool is bought 'in the grease', in its natural state, or having been scoured to remove grease. Next is the blending process, during which fatty acid oil is put back into the wool to protect the fibre. After that, the wool can be spun then dyed to one

Ebley Mill and the weir. (Photograph courtesy of Jack Marshall)

colour or dyed, blended and the yarns mixed. We could do either at Ebley, but in the main it was more economical to make coloured yarns, and it gave the designer more scope. The wool is then carded: the wool fibre is combed, then wound onto spools and transported into a spinning mule, which in turn spins the yarn. You then give your designer a free hand to work out the weave, subject to customer requirements.

When the cloth has been woven, it must be repaired to remove imperfections, and knots: this is carried out by burlers and menders, who sit at sloping tables, picking out any foreign bodies and breaking off knots. This skill takes years to learn.

The cloth is then sent for scouring and milling: it is put into a washer and runs round in a long chain. It is rinsed, then tentered, or dried. In the old days it would be tentered outside on hooks and stretched. It was a common sight to see rows and rows of cloth on the hillsides, and each clothier had his own mark, which would be woven into either end of the fabric. It was a truth mark and it protected the goods on the tenterhooks.

The cloth is then taken to the dry finishing department, where it is left to stand for seventy-two hours, having been sprayed with a fine mist of water to return it to its natural condition. This process is called decatising. There are a variety of ways to finish: you can lift the fibres to raise a fluffy nap or raise it and then cut off the nap. A machine with hollow rollers then presses the cloth: the steam passes through it and the cloth comes out completely flat. The steam and the pressure give sheen to the fabric. The cloth is finally folded and despatched to the customers.

The internal pillars of Stanley Mill, its flagstone and brick floors. The iron for the pillars came from Benjamin Gibbon of the Earl of Leicester's Level New Foundry, Dudley. They were transported by canal from the Midland foundry. Note the double-iron fire doors at the far end; there was another identical pair on the other side. The top of every casting bolted onto an identical set of cast pillars on the floor above. (Photograph courtesy of Jack Marshall)

six

Campaigns

Council leadership

Everyone has a vision for their own town. The fact is that these visions can never be realised without the leadership of the local council. Whilst this chapter focuses on the projects which have not happened, people may be sufficiently magnanimous to give Stroud District Council the credit for projects which have succeeded in the town. These include the Leisure Centre, Brunel Mall car park and the Museum in the Park. Soon to come to fruition are the restoration of the Stroudwater Canal and the town's new cinema. None of these would have happened without SDC's leadership.

Stroud District Council, 2004

Stroud campaign against the Ring Road (SCAR), 1975

The best site of any town in the Cotswolds

I am a Senior Lecturer in History and Theory of Art at the University of Gloucestershire, Cheltenham. I arrived in Stroud with my family from Cheltenham in a snowstorm in January in 1973. The ring road controversy started in late 1975 and the public inquiry was in 1976. It was all very interesting.

I became involved through Mike Goodenough. In those days he was a long-haired student at the College of Technology in Cheltenham and I had been a long-haired lecturer at the same place. He and his wife Joy had mounted an exhibition in the Shambles, which I visited, and I started talking to them. They told me about the proposals for the ring road. I saw an artist's reconstruction, which was so horrific I decided to get involved. I met the early campaign organisers, Claire Toy and Mary Fermor, along with a wonderfully disparate group of 'Stroudies' who were equally incensed. Peter Minall, the vicar of

the parish church, was persuaded to become our chairman. We had lots of meetings, often late into the night, and we took over a rather rundown 'office space' in Swan Lane, cleaned it up, painted it and used it as the SCAR (Stroud Campaign Against the Ring Road) headquarters.

We had many debates about the issues with other groups. I remember presenting our case to the Stroud Chamber of Commerce and the villagers of Amberley, who were kind enough to invite Claire Toy and myself. At the latter I enjoyed myself enormously by debating the issue with Desmond Harper, who was the chairman of the Stroud District Council, and a committed advocate of the ring road as, inexplicably, were so many councillors. Only the Liberals were on our side. I used to take a painted cardboard model, made by Peter Waller, of the proposed ring road around with me, which showed the proposed layout. We thought it was going to be the Spaghetti Junction of the Cotswolds! The evidence from the model only confirms this.

Many listed buildings would have been lost. A serviceable group of homes in Locking Hill had already been demolished, where the surgery now sits. The old police station and British School would have gone; there would have been a stilted section of the road over the Slad Road and a 1:10 section going uphill from there to the Cross. About half a dozen listed shops, including the so-called Medieval Hall where Bishopston Trading is now, would also go. The road would have run just six feet from the museum and fifteen feet, at most, from the Reading Room of the Library. 'We'll give them double glazing', they said! A 1:10 hill! Lansdown was to be blocked at this point by the ring road but for a pedestrian passageway, ideal for muggers and those taken short. The road was never to have been more than a two-lane highway, although there had to be a third 'crawler' lane just for lorries. We were

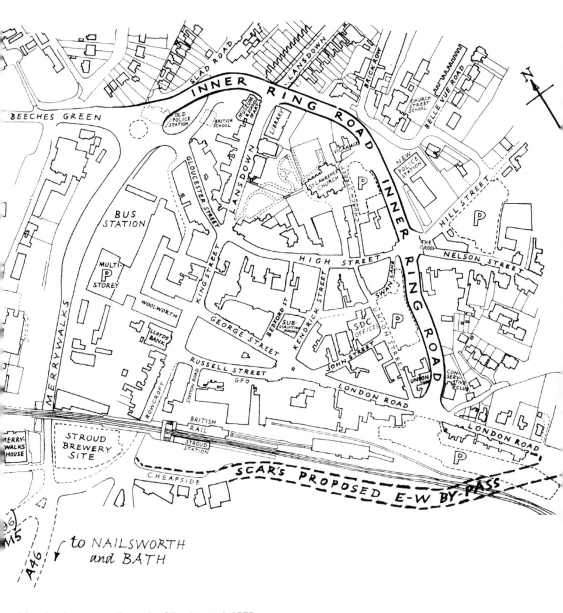

Map showing prospective route of the ring road, 1975.

told that 'in principle' it was a twenty-four-foot carriageway, which caused much amusement. Heavy goods vehicles would have been constantly grinding up that hill, that's why it was so wide all the way along: it was about thirty-two feet at its narrowest at the top of the town and then there would have been another 1:10 hill all the way back down. A retired meteorologist volunteered evidence as to the pollution that would occur – and next to a school!

We formed different working groups: one looked at the technology of the road and alternatives; one looked at the legal and environmental issues. I was involved in publicity with Claire Toy and others and we occupied the Swan Lane office where we had the model and photographs and artists impressions. We got a petition together and marched to Gloucester to present it at Shire Hall.

We lost. The County Council voted against us, but we said 'bugger it' and carried on because there was absolutely no argument for the ring road at all. This was early in 1976.

The opposition, Conservative and Labour councillors and others, organised their own petition. They said they wanted to get the traffic out of Stroud and away from the centre, but they didn't want it too far away. They said the ring road would give a nice view of Stroud and people would be attracted in. They didn't mention that traffic would be funnelled from the Cross, down the High Street, down Union Street and onto a car park where the Cornhill development stands! They also said there would be a nice view of Rodborough from the ring road! They really thought they were solving a problem.

Anthony Kershaw was the local Tory MP at the time. He was a lawyer and he saw that we had the right to an inquiry. He was the person who got it for us. I remember him coming to the offices in his fawn coat. He was a bit of a hero really.

We were very fortunate to have a local solicitor, Martin Green, on our side who presented a good image on our behalf as he led the attack, because he was so very gentlemanly, charming and polite. We had a public inquiry, which finished in late October 1976. We didn't have the result until two and a quarter years later! We had won!

One of our group, a retired schoolteacher, Ruby Court, had done a wonderful painting of the ring road, very Beryl Cook-like, with the cars zooming around, very exaggerated, and we turned it into a card, then later, when we had won, Claire printed a tyre track across it saying 'cancelled' and sent it out as an invitation to a big celebration party. A cake was made specially with 'Ring Road RIP' on it and some of us, dressed as undertakers, carried it very solemnly into the party and cut it up.

We felt vindicated, especially when we read in Mr Jeremiah's report that he considered that the ring road would have been 'an environmental disaster'. It was the sort of report we would have written ourselves! I immediately became a member of the Civic Society, which was a good society but which needed geeing up. I then became chairman in 1978, with Nigel Shaw (who had shown Mr Jeremiah that we didn't need the ring road) as secretary. I was chairman until 1985 when Mike Hill took over, followed by Julian Usborne and then the present chair, Juliet Shipman. All except Mike were 'outsiders', but all of us could see the enormous potential of Stroud. It still seems to me to have the best site of any town in the Cotswolds, almost like an Italian hill town, though the SDC still does its best to hide this.

Alan Ford

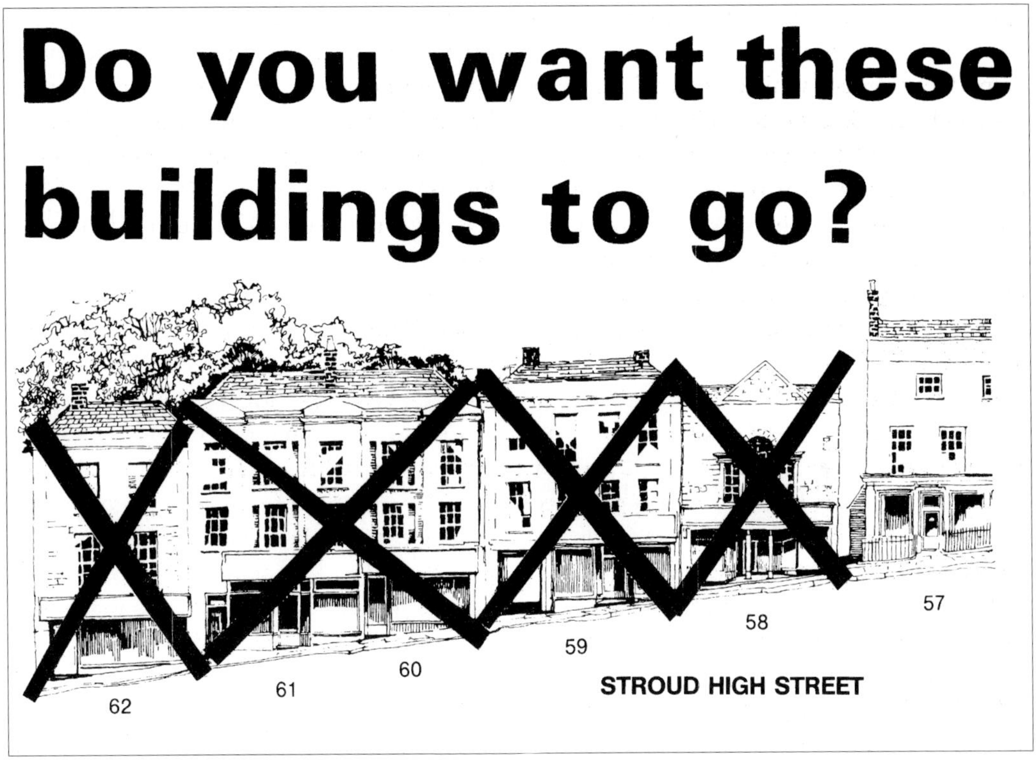

Do you want these buildings to go?

57
58
59
60
61
62

STROUD HIGH STREET

Stroud High Street poster by Terry Thomas, 1980.

Stroud High Street Action Group (SHSAG), 1980

The newcomers to Stroud find their voice

When we first moved here from Oxfordshire in 1972, Stroud and the surrounding area pleasantly surprised me. I remember going to Stroud, driving along Merrywalks and seeing the old police station and I remember saying to my wife, 'If anyone ever tries to pull that building down, I'm going to leave'. I just loved it instantly and was totally horrified when, six months later, it was all boarded up ready to be demolished! Stroud District Council had this brilliant idea of putting a new road slap through the middle of Stroud. The Inner Ring Road was to run from Merrywalks, knocking down the old police station and the British School, round the corner, wind its way up the hill to Lewis's, the electrical shop at the top of Stroud, cut across the top of the High Street, knocking down another six listed buildings and all the way back down again to the London Road. The new police station was being built at the time. The Cross was the heart of the town, but some of it had already been knocked down.

This outraged a Stroud lady called Clare Toy and she started SCAR: Stroud Campaign Against the Ring Road. The campaign fought for a public inquiry, which they got, but it took the Secretary of State two years to find in their favour. The council got a real bloody nose, but it showed that the people had some power; the newcomers to Stroud had found their voice.

The 'Coffin Protest' through Stroud, May 1980.

The story goes on: in 1976 I rented out a small cottage to a man called Tom Bermingham. Tom had found that there were five derelict buildings in Stroud High Street, owned by Milwards, the shoe shop. Milwards wanted to knock them down and had put in for planning in 1976. The council turned down the planning application and at that point, Tom, who was concerned about the unemployed, approached Milwards with an idea to rent one of the buildings for the benefit of the community. He set up a café called Starters, applied for grants and gave work to the unemployed. Starters Café became a real focus for the community.

The buildings had been empty for four years between 1976 and 1980. The council became concerned about them and served a Dangerous Structures Notice on them, part of the 1936 Public Health Act. This notice gave Milwards the opportunity to repair the buildings, or they would be demolished within three months. Therefore, by simply neglecting the buildings, Milwards had achieved their original aim.

At this point I started organising demonstrations: we carried a coffin around the town protesting against this decision. Tom and I and several others moved into the building, we squatted and sat there knowing that it was only a matter of time, that it was coming to the end of the three-month period and that there would be a confrontation.

Rooftop protesters, May 1980.

Sure enough there was. At about 10.30 a.m. on Wednesday 14 May 1980, four demolition men arrived and began pulling off the slates. There was a rooftop tussle between twenty-five protesters and four demolition men; we sat on the roof. The council were doubly worried: one, that the building would fall into the street and two, we would go with it! They closed the High Street on Thursday while further talks took place. There were banner headlines, 'Siege in the High Street!' The siege finally came to an end on Friday night when we were granted an injunction halting the demolition. The following Tuesday, the council brought in a couple of old dustcarts to either end of the High Street blocking the, street again claiming that the listed buildings were a public danger.

Three of us, Steve Tomlin, Mike Goodenough and I, went to see a lawyer called Peter Hankins in Stroud who said that there were two Acts of Parliament, Planning and Public Health, which were directly in conflict with each other: this could be challenged in the High Court. We started SHSAG (Stroud High Street Action Group) and we produced a newsletter and had meetings at Starters Café. I agreed to fund it. We went up to the High Court and took out an action for Judicial Review. The judges, Lord Donaldson and Lord Woolf asked Stroud District Council to reconsider its decision to serve its demolition notice. Unfortunately,

The dustcarts put in place at either end of the High Street by Stroud District Council.

the council decided they weren't going to budge. There were long delays and it came to a public inquiry. The law established that the two Acts were in conflict but that the listed building legislation took precedence over the public health: it was established in law and set a precedent.

We just thought that Stroud was worth preserving. If you look at some of the old paintings of Stroud it was as pretty as Painswick, but Stroud had the doubtful advantage of access for transport, which in its turn spelt progress. For some time, the council had been pulling the old buildings down and putting up new ones. That would have been fine if the new ones being built had any kind of quality, but the precinct had been built and we saw the potential for ruin. To many Stroud people these five buildings in the High Street were an eyesore; they had been allowed to deteriorate so much that the local people wanted to tear them down. At one point there was a plan to knock down the whole of one half of the High Street and open it up to the church!

We had a victory and the buildings were maintained and they are still there in the High Street today.

Julian Usborne

Outsiders?

When we moved to Stroud in 1974 it felt like the closest you could get to Ireland without crossing the sea! Everybody seemed to move around at half speed; I thought it was terrific. Lots of other people moved from Cheltenham at about the same time: John and Maggie Mills, for example.

My first involvement as a 'protester' was with Claire Toy and Mary Fermor over a spat with the council, who wanted to remove the children's playground from Stratford Park. Joy and I had a small child at the time and we weren't having it.

Claire Toy was one of those rare people about whom I have never heard anyone say a bad word. When she withdrew from campaigning I was very sad. She was a great lady, amazingly energetic, and she had that rare ability to make everybody feel involved.

Towards the end of the High Street campaign, we found drawings and models, which showed that the County Council had had grand plans to literally demolish the place, including the whole of the Lansdown side of the High Street. The police station and the bus station had been built in the 1960s, but the rest of the proposed redevelopment was still sitting, waiting on file. Stroud was then about ten years behind everywhere else in most things and, as well as being part of its charm, that is what saved the town, really. By the time the battle for the High Street began, our previous experience in SCAR and the support of other organisations meant that we were much better able to resist, than if it had happened earlier.

The greatest change in public opinion that I have ever witnessed came with the ring road. The scale of the road was hard to envisage: if you looked at the plan it looked like a little road and many people thought that it was good idea but what they couldn't do was to see the impact it was going to have on the town. The old police station would have been demolished and in its place there would have been a huge flyover, twenty or thirty feet above the ground. One Saturday morning in 1976, we trooped out and put up aluminium poles marked with its height all the way along to illustrate this. People's jaws dropped; they simply couldn't conceive the idea. I think the argument was won at that point.

But we were still outsiders. I don't think we ever shook that off; it didn't matter whether you won the arguments, you were still an outsider. How could we possibly think we could just turn up here and tell people what ought to be done? What right did we have to do that?

Protesters outside the threatened High Street buildings, May 1980. Steve Tomlin has the microphone.

I became involved in the High Street campaign when I walked into town one morning in 1980 to buy a loaf of bread. Steve Tomlin – I don't know whether he was with or without megaphone, but it rarely made any difference – had just painted some of the derelict buildings, to show what they could look like. After speaking to Steve, I thought that the demolition of these historic buildings couldn't be allowed to happen.

During the campaign, I focused on the legal and planning issues, which I found both fascinating and empowering. The attractive thing about the legal process is that you argue your case in front of people who will hear it dispassionately. Particularly in the case of planning issues and public inquiries: everything gets dragged out and it is terribly time-consuming and expensive, but it does give the full facts a proper hearing.

Ours was a simple issue; it just needed a hugely expensive High Court action to sort it out. The legal case was about resolving the council's claim that they could issue a demolition notice on a listed building. We challenged that claim and said that it was

Protestors in Stroud High Street.

absurd: a Dangerous Structure Notice couldn't possibly take precedence over a listing.

The High Court found that the council had failed to consider all the powers available to them, and in so doing, created a legal precedent. In their judgement, Lords Donaldson and Woolf directed Stroud District Council to reconsider their position. SDC responded by allowing the limited demolition of the dangerous part of one building, leaving the fate of the rest to be decided by a public inquiry. Their Lordships' judgement, together with SDC's unexpectedly imaginative response, effectively put a stop to this sort of nationwide abuse of listed buildings.

Barely recovered from the court case we then had to prepare for a public inquiry, in which we had to demonstrate that the restoration and conversion of these buildings was economically viable. Steve made a major contribution during the public inquiry because he was working as a developer and understood that side of things.

Although Julian Usborne, Steve Tomlin and I were often seen as the public face of the campaign, it could not have succeeded without the time, effort and commitment of a great many people. While the three of us were forced to use our homes as security during the court case, many others were no less prepared to put themselves on the line. Those who occupied the rooftops for instance put their safety, as well as their livelihoods, at risk.

In common with all the other Stroud campaigns a vast amount of work had to be done behind the scenes. Evidence had to be collected, newsletters produced, endless meetings held, children minded, benefit gigs organised, funds raised –seemingly endless tasks, but always someone ready to do them. I wish I could mention all these people here, but they know who they are, and hopefully they realise how important their contributions were.

We were also extremely fortunate to have the support of local solicitor Peter Hankins, who helped us, at a much-reduced rate, as did a number of other planning and building professionals. And of course, without Julian agreeing to underwrite the entire campaign, we could not have proceeded at all.

At the time I saw what we were doing as addressing a certain kind of conservatism, but it just seems to have been replaced by a different sort. You can't now touch even the most boring or inconsequential listed building, without going through the most elaborate and ridiculous bureaucratic dance. The innovative, energy-efficient conversion of old buildings still seems beyond our grasp.

In the end though it wasn't just about saving listed buildings, it was about encouraging people to take an active interest in determining the future of their environment: for things not to happen by default.

Mike Goodenough

Save Our Stroud Trees (SOST), 1989

A great triumph

I was born and bred in Bermondsey. Jennifer and I were doing residential work running children's homes and we ended up looking for the place with the smallest number of staff and we eventually found No. 28 Lansdown in 1978 – an eight-bed unit for teenagers leaving local authority care. We arrived about a week before the result of the ring road campaign was announced. We were present for the rejoicing but we didn't really know much about that.

I used to go to lots of Stroud District Council meetings, because in 1985 the council proposed a supermarket development in Cornhill, in the centre of town. Council offices occupied a large part of the site, which they wanted to sell to a developer. I have never liked supermarkets anyway and did not want one in town. Nobody has ever asked me whether I wanted a supermarket; it just seemed to be a question of 'which one?' So that's what started me 'council watching': how do these proposals become so advanced, without us townspeople knowing anything?

In mid-December 1988, Bob Eccles, a councillor, alerted Veronica Wood that some trees on Stratford Road were under threat. There were thirty-two trees to be felled, the aim being to widen and straighten the road, nominally to improve access to the brand-new Tesco store. In fact, a road-widening scheme had been on file at Gloucestershire County Council since the '60s. By the time we heard about the plans, the officers told us it was too late, as the parkland had already been sold to Tesco. Tesco had been happy to buy the Stratford Park land from the council for £385,000 because it meant they could get their store open, and the council was very happy because it made the park worth about a million pounds an acre.

The first phase of our 'Save The Trees' campaign was the letter-writing phase: writing to Tesco, to councillors and trying to whip up support through the press. We asked Stroud District Council to 'stop the felling of the beautiful mature trees bordering Stratford Park...and give consideration to alternative plans which will improve road safety without damaging the local environment.'

In February 1989, between 600 and 700 people marched in support of the campaign to save the trees, after which the council compromised and decided to fell only thirteen trees: six beech and one hornbeam in front of the tennis courts on Stratford Road and below that, seven more.

Campaigners twice stopped these trees being felled by the council, on two separate Sunday mornings in May 1989, after which Tesco said they would not fell the trees 'against the wishes of the community'. Weeks went by

and eventually, in August, another attempt was made by the council to fell the trees. This time, it was at midnight and there was a great deal of aggravation, as protesters were pulled away from the trees, again and again, by a group of untrained Bristol security guards. The protest continued all night until eventually, at 5.30 a.m., the police called off the operation in the interests of safety.

From that moment on we decided we had to mount a guard on the trees, twenty-four hours a day. Steve Tomlin built a platform and we occupied the trees until October: fifty-six days and nights. The trees were roped for easy climbing and wrapped in chainsaw-proof wire mesh to prevent any surprise attempt at ring barking. Steel hawsers connected all the trees, thirty feet above the ground, so that no tree could be felled while still attached to the others. But it was beginning to get cold and it was more difficult to get people out there in numbers. We had a minimum of two people at a time doing four-hour shifts during the day, and then we had the night shift until eight the following morning. People slept up the trees, where it was thought they would be safe from marauders. Sometimes you got yobs coming past drunk, and campaigners did get attacked in the trees one night.

It was wonderful: people turned out physically, whenever they were needed, rain or shine: a complete cross section of people, many of them Stroud born and bred. People such as Sue Hinch, Pamela and Brian Dean and Bob and Marilyn Alliss: they were among the most reliable members of the campaign. They were fantastic, and continue to be. Very few members of the campaign had ever been in confrontation with authority before, but they all knew the road scheme, which required the felling of the trees, was wrong. I never felt any different from these people; the only division I felt was entirely between the council and the general public. But as the campaign went on, people did drift away from supporting the trees, because they were generally fed up. They wanted it sorted. I think that they wanted to hear something else on the radio, so we did lose support as the months went by.

We continued to seek help: we had experts in to prove the trees still had a lot of life in them, that there was no problem with them. Completely independently and without us knowing, the *Western Daily Press* commissioned a chap from London University, John Adams, a geographer who specialises in what constitutes risk. They paid for him to come and do an assessment on the trees and the council's proposals. His findings were that it would be much more dangerous to make the alterations than to leave things as they were. The *Western Daily Press* became a fantastic supporter over a period of months. They gave us a lot of coverage, leader articles and so on; it didn't do us any harm.

By degrees and in the end, things went our way. We knew we had won by the beginning of January 1990. Over the Christmas period, the Stroud District Council, which had become totally isolated over the whole affair, had drawn up its own scheme, which was the same as ours all along. Their barrister had advised them that if they went to the appeal (arranged fourteen months after the start) they would lose hands down. So, on 9 January, they reversed all previous decisions and put forward their own plan; the next day Tesco said they were happy to accept it and the day after that, the public inquiry opened: so that's how much of a cliffhanger it was.

One of the great triumphs is not just that the trees have been saved, but that the number of traffic accidents in the area has halved. That might only be a relatively small number, perhaps four or five people who have not had an accident, but it is important in human terms.

Ron Birch

Ron Birch also went on, with others, to save the hornbeam tree on the forecourt of the Subscription Rooms, threatened with felling by the SDC in June 1998.

The great tree siege

I had been involved in the past in issues which had gained prominence in Stroud. It was August 1989 and I was running an architectural salvage yard near Painswick when I received a call to say that there was a lot of hire equipment being put on standby for the Stroud District Council, ready for something to happen at the Leisure Centre. People were appearing from nowhere. We were told that the local authority had employed a company and a lot of unemployed people from Bristol. We alerted others. The word spread; Stroud campaigners had developed a good network after their experience in the ring road and High Street protests. Tesco had been underway as a project on the site of the old Townsend's Seed Store on Stratford Road and there was a quiet, almost forlorn, acceptance of its inevitability. The council wanted to improve the access to the supermarket and there had already been two unsuccessful, Sunday morning attempts to fell a fine row of semi-mature beech trees. These late-night Bristol sub-contractors had been engaged by Stroud District Council, under the control of their official Mike Snell.

There was a really emotive reaction to the secrecy and there was a huge turnout. It was after dark and no one knew what was going to happen. Contractors appeared and began to erect picket fences. Mike Snell explained that it was necessary to erect this *cordon sanitaire*, but would say no more. One thing fed on another and there was a lot of drama. By mid-evening there was a stand-off and the police had arrived. There was a lot of shouting and screaming when it emerged that the intention was to bring the trees down. We confronted the unemployed people working for the sub-contractors and many of them withdrew. The crowd was getting bigger; the word had spread like wildfire.

Pamela Dean turned up and brought others, the Green Lobby and the Labour Party was there. Then there came a crunch at about 10.30 p.m. The stand-off had gone on too long and Mike Snell asked the contractors to go ahead and put the fence up. As fast as they did, we took it down. The contractors were getting agitated and the police intervened. They decided they wanted to clear the area saying it was a health and safety issue. They told everyone to go home, but it was obvious that they had crossed the line and although they were trying to be neutral, they were actually going to allow the whole thing to go ahead.

I have climbed regularly and I knew about prussic knots; I borrowed some scarves and made loops of them, tied them tightly into a ring and fed them round a telegraph pole. I climbed a telegraph pole with power cables on it. I found one that was close to the trees. I was obscured until I was at the top. The police demanded that I got down, but I knew if I came down, the trees would come down.

The police then demanded the contractor withdrew, and gave categorical assurances that they would not allow any activity on the site until matters were properly discussed. That was the beginning of the great tree siege.

Ron Birch and Pamela Dean were among the leading lights of the Save Our Stroud Trees campaign and it was ordained that we should maintain a vigil there. I went with my son and built a tree house in one of the beech trees. We slept there every night for five or six weeks. I recall on Friday nights you used to have to suffer the tirade of drunks coming out of the pubs and there were one or two quite ugly

confrontations. But we survived and history tells us that we were successful and we were successful because we used common sense.

Over the weeks that followed, SDC maintained that Tesco could not open without an improved road system. If they failed to open, Tesco would sue the local authority. SDC said they would be in default of their contractual agreement with Tesco.

We formed a powerful and well-organised pressure group with the experience that had been gained in protests such as the High Street. We were able to mount a sustained campaign and demonstrate that Tesco, at no point, had insisted on these road changes and that SDC were very much the ones who had promoted this idea. We made the point that if they widened the road at that point, it would become a racetrack and therefore much less safe anyway, thereby contradicting their intentions.

The local authority tried to prove that the trees were in a poor state; we proved that they were extremely virile and had another twenty years in them! The whole thing was mixed up and badly thought through.

We spoke to people in Tesco at the highest level; we knew that Tesco was flexible and expressed a desire to avoid confrontation. The planning authority was Stroud District Council, but the highways authority was the County Council and they did not want to change anything; they were quite happy to put yellow lines, traffic calming, whatever, but it wasn't a big issue. So Stroud District Council found themselves isolated and in conflict with the County Council. They had a client contractual arrangement with Tesco to ensure that the store opened on time which was less than watertight and they had inept officers, who with a little bit of subtlety could have avoided all conflict.

It went from being a parish issue to something much bigger. The local paper supported

Above: Steve Tomlin protests from the treetop.

Left: Steve Tomlin, 2004. (Photograph by Peta Bunbury)

our case very well and the television companies found it irresistible. The council came across as inflexible and badly informed, whilst we retained a great deal of popular public support.

We brought in a tree surgeon from Germany and expert in transplanting trees – that was ruled out because they were too mature. We continually examined options and ideas, and in the end the resolution was self-evident: to put a footpath inside the Leisure Centre taking the pavement away from the road and to widen the road by about two or three feet. The number of accidents has been halved and we've retained the trees. In the end, Tesco told the council that they would sue unless they were allowed to open on time, with a road system that they and the County Council were entirely happy with. Stroud District Council were left to back down; also, public opinion had been working on the district councillors and one by one they pulled their support away. In the end they had no option but to concede. We took legal advice and we demonstrated that they had not examined the full range of alternative planning options. They failed to understand the public mood and were in the end destroyed by their own inflexibility.

In many towns it would have been a non-event, but not in Stroud. The trees became symbolic and they gave a focal point for community politics.

Steve Tomlin

The Hill Paul Regeneration Group, 2000

Part of living in Stroud

I started off life in the North of England where I met my husband Gordon, and I've been teaching most of my life. We moved to this area in the 1960s and we've been here ever since apart from a brief time in Cornwall.

I think I am typical of many people in the area in that whenever we went to London on the train we would see the Hill Paul building; whenever we went about our daily business we would see it and it always symbolised home. It was part of living in Stroud, part of me.

I'd been a member of Stroud Civic Society for quite some time and on 23 November 2000, Mike Hill, son of Ken Hill, was giving a lecture on buildings in Stroud in the 1950s; buildings which had all been demolished. For the last few minutes he moved away from the main theme of the talk and told us that he thought we ought to know about the Hill Paul building. He put up a picture on the screen and told us that it had been scheduled for demolition. My husband and I looked at each other; we had been involved in the High Street Action Group and we knew what Stroud District Council was capable of doing. So I talked to two or three people there, asked if they were interested in helping save it and arranged a meeting.

After the first meeting, we had another one, which we opened to the public and we formed the Hill Paul Regeneration Group. We stood in the High Street and collected signatures on Christmas cards saying, 'There's still time' which we sent to the owner of the building, Malcolm Bushell, urging him to reprieve the building. He said later that they made an enormous impact on him.

It was January 2001: the developers were threatening to move the bulldozers onto the site; there were demonstrations; group member Eddie Cook single-handedly fooled the wrecking crew by wearing lots of different hats to persuade the authorities that others were in the building, climbing on to the roof and draping the dramatic message 'Save Me' down the front of Hill Paul.

We had more protests and many meetings. Bushell had a change of heart and we got the chance to buy the site. We needed to form a limited company: eventually eight directors came forward and put up the necessary money for the £65,000 deposit. The deal was that we had to pay £1.3 million within the year, and if we didn't find the money by January 2002, we would lose our deposit and the building would go back to the developer.

We made a shopping list of what we would all like to see in the building: everybody wanted a café on the top floor; we wanted art galleries, a crèche, alternative health clinics, a cinema and other wonderful ideas.

We got the first lot of money then we paid the next month and the next, but after that I knew we couldn't raise the money and that it was essential to find a developer who would preserve the building.

This is when the group split. There were two sets of campaigners, the Company and the Group. The Group wanted to go the community-based, charitable route, which involved getting funding from ethical banks and grants from the Regional Development Agency. One or two people stayed with the Group and the Company. But basically the Company were able to make decisions and the Group felt they had lost control. The Group thought that the Company members were traitors by going to developers, and although I shared their dreams for Hill Paul, for me, it had become a question of finding a developer who would simply save the building.

Eventually in January 2002, after months of talking to various developers, we secured a deal with Chelbury Homes to turn the building into flats and the agreement was that they preserved Hill Paul. That was the bottom line. The original aim was achieved: the building was saved. It was worth all the aggro. I always liked the building.

Irene Hopwood

The councillor

We would be in clover now, had we not pulled down the Almshouses, the Georgian listed building in the High Street, the housing up Cornhill and had we not put up the police station or Merrywalks. I was involved in the Stroud campaigns, in the two public inquiries, but I am the only one left who has come through as a councillor. The others who were active through the 1970s and '80s have become tired of campaigning. But how long *can* people do it? How long can they keep protesting? Most people live busy lives; issues only become important when it's too late. In local government, because of the current system, where backbenchers have less and less influence, it needs real determination to keep involved in the decision-making, whichever political party you belong to.

Councillor John Marjoram

seven

In the News

From reporter to editor

The Air Ministry went back to London after the war. I didn't want to go and live in London but I didn't know what to do. My father picked up the *Stroud Journal* and said, 'Oh look, the newspaper wants to recruit a reporter'. I was discharged from war duties in August 1944 with pleurisy and I started at the *Journal* in October the same year. The pay was £2 a week, with the promise of an extra five shillings after five weeks. I got the five shillings sure enough, but I signed no indentures and didn't know whether they were gong to keep me on. I learned shorthand at Miss Smith's school of typing, but never really learned to type properly; I still type with two fingers.

I had no journalistic experience and they threw me in at the deep end by sending me to cover a funeral. In those days, you went and took the people's names at the beginning then you went round to the cemetery and took names from the wreaths. Later you went to the house for details about the person who had died. It was important to get your report in the same week otherwise the *Stroud News* would beat you to it! I remember going to a funeral in Forest Green and crying my eyes out because it was for a young woman who had died in childbirth. I'm a sentimental person and I always get upset: even if I see the Queen going through London and everyone cheering, I get a tear in my eye! My father was the same; it runs in the family.

Dennis Mason at Buckingham Palace to receive his MBE in 1988, with his wife Muriel and their children Paul and Carole.

The competition between the two papers was terrific. The *Stroud Journal* was founded in 1852, supporting the Liberal cause, while the *Stroud News* was more Conservative and sold mostly in Painswick and Minchinhampton. In the 1930s the *Journal* was taken over by the Bailey Organisation who pumped money into the paper. The *Stroud News* just couldn't continue and we amalgamated in 1957. The *Journal*'s Editor, Mr Geoffrey Saunders, became the overall Editor and my colleague Jack Sollars became News Editor. I was Sports Editor, then News Editor for four years and Editor for ten. The *Stroud News and Journal* was always based in Lansdown and still is.

I was awarded the MBE in 1978. Some members of staff nominated me, but I always said it was awarded to the staff. I can honestly say that no one left the *News and Journal* office because they fell out with me.

Dennis Mason, born 1925

A royal visit

Princess Elizabeth came to Stroud in March 1950. She had visited the Wildfowl and Wetlands Trust at Slimbridge in the morning and came on to Stroud by train. She got off at Stroud and they had a red carpet from the station to the Imperial. Mr Fred Daniels, Managing Director of Daniels and Chairman of the Council, met the Princess. Mrs Birt, a nurse at Stroud Hospital for many years, presented her with a bouquet of flowers. Her and her husband, Bert Birt, were the licensees for the Fountain along Slad Road for many years. Mrs Birt was well known at Stroud Hospital and she was a councillor. There is still a plaque commemorating the event in the Imperial Hotel today.

David Russell, born 1939

Big welcome prepared at Stroud

A considerable time before Princess Elizabeth was due to arrive in Stroud for her eagerly awaited visit, crowds began to gather in the streets, people having evidently decided to have an early lunch in order to be able to secure the best points of vantage along the route that the royal car would travel on the way from visiting the Severn Wild Fowl Trust at Slimbridge.

Most of the shops in the centre of the town were closed at 2 p.M. For an hour in order that the staff could join the crowds waiting with unconcealed excitement to see the heir to the throne.

More than an hour before the princess reached the town the central part had become uncomfortably crowded and as the time drew nearer, the streets became densely packed with people all eager to show their affection and loyalty to the royal visitor.

The Citizen, Saturday 4 March 1950

Down Your Way, Sunday 6 January 1952

In 1952, pre-television days, the BBC radio programme *Down Your Way* presented by Richard Dimbleby, came to Stroud. He first interviewed Mr James Stuart Daniels in his office in Lightpill then went on to speak to Mr R. Bashford from Strachan's; Mr Sandling a basket-maker from Dudbridge; Revd H.D. Woolcott, rector of Woodchester, who spoke about the Roman Pavement; Mr and Mrs C.D. Knapton - he was a well-known cyclist and she had given long service at Arthur's Press, Woodchester. Also interviewed were Mr R.S. Grover, Works Manager at Stroud Piano Company, Mr S. Townsend, blind organist and local entertainer, Mrs I. Hurlbatt, secretary of Stroud Valley Community Centre Ladies' Choir, Mr F.W. Stevens, manager of Midland Fisheries, Nailsworth, a Mrs Ivy Card, a Mr H. Bassett and Mr D. Gardiner.

The musical requests were mainly classical, but there were a couple of contemporary tunes. I remember there was a show running

Her Royal Highness Princess Elizabeth on a visit to the Severn Wildfowl Trust at Slimbridge in March 1950, before visiting Stroud. Pictured here with Commander Peter Scott, being shown a tame badger. (Photograph courtesy of Lady Scott)

in London at the time called, *Our Miss Phoebe'* a love story, and there was a song in it called 'I Leave My Heart in an English Garden'; that was the request of Mr Sandling. Mr Bassett's choice was 'Underneath the Arches' by Flanagan and Allen and Mrs Hurlbatt chose 'I'll See You Again' by Peggy Wood and George Metaxa.

We were on our way back from school to dinner at home and Richard Dimbleby was in his car, and he stopped and asked my father

the way to the Bear at Rodborough. We went back to school and said we'd seen Richard Dimbleby.

David Russell, born 1939

Mr Laurie Lee, MBE
Included in the New Year's Honours List was the award of MBE to Mr L.E.A. (Laurie) Lee for his work as staff caption writer for the Festival of Britain office. In this manner, public acknowledgement

John V. Smith, in his England shirt, at Victory Park, Cainscross, the week after his first international rugby match, England v. Wales at Twickenham, in January 1950.

is made of the brilliant and unusual literary career of a young man who was brought up at The Slad and received his education at the Stroud Central School.

Stroud Journal, Friday 4 January 1952

From Stroud to Twickenham

While I was in the Army I used to come back to Stroud to play rugby. In my first game for Stroud Rugby Club, I was centre three-quarter with Charlie Barnett and Martin Cullimore. Both men had been offered professional forms but Cullimore's father had asked him to choose between being a professional sportsman or taking on the family farm. He chose the farm.

The Marling and Evans cricket team, which defeated the *Chance of a Lifetime* film crew team, summer 1949. Jack is in the back row, fourth from the left.

We beat Bridgwater at Bridgwater; my first game for Stroud. I scored a try and we won the match. That was the beginning of my association with Stroud Rugby Club. After that somebody must have seen me in the County team and I got picked for the County 1947/48 season. I was in the Army and coming back on vacation and playing for Stroud and I got picked to play centre three-quarter for the Army at Twickenham in the same season. The following season I went up to Cambridge and, in 1949/50, I played for England.

John V. Smith, born 1926

Stroud Player on Wing for England

J.V. Smith of Stroud and Cambridge University has got his England Rugby cap. But he has been selected to play on the wing and a surprise is the exclusion of another Gloucestershire man, Jack Gregory.

Smith and Gregory formed the right wing in Saturday's final trial and the Stroud man's quickness off the mark to take advantage of the openings made by Ivor Preece seemed to show that he would be at his best playing next to the captain. However, the selectors have put him in the place of the schoolboy Hyda.

The Citizen, Monday 9 January 1950

The chance of a lifetime

Chance of a Lifetime was filmed at Stanley Mill in 1949 and my job was to stop the crew and extras playing parts in the film from getting their hands in the machinery! I was also responsible for making sure everyone kept on working when there wasn't a film star looking over his or her shoulder! Bernard Miles, Basil Radford, Patrick Troughton, Kenneth More, Hattie Jacques and Sam Kydd were all in the film. The cast list now reads like an obituary.

Jack Marshall

The Meningitis Trust

I was just an ordinary parent

In December 1984, I was an ordinary parent with a baby girl, Rachael, and a two-year-old son, Dan. But then, at Christmas, Dan became very ill. There had been several cases of meningitis in the Stroud Valleys, but we never thought that's what it could be. Two doctors and three home visits later, he was eventually admitted to Gloucester Royal Hospital. Dan was there for two weeks and they gave him the antibiotics and told me it was HIB Meningitis. I said, very naively, 'Is that the Stroud strain?' They said no. I was so ignorant as a parent.

In March there were several other cases in the area and people were starting to get panicky. The headlines were, 'No Need for Concern'. This made me so angry; I was sitting there with my child, three months on, OK he was not dead, but he was still a very sick child. There were loads of problems with him that weren't there before and there was no help, even though as a family we needed support.

So, I wrote to the Editor of the *Stroud News and Journal*, Dennis Mason, and he said he thought my story should make front-page news. Steve Tomlin, who was a District Councillor at the time, had just moved on to our estate and came to see me and said he was very interested in the whole case. He had the contacts and wanted to help.

A public meeting was called. I was interested in Steve's facts about meningitis, that the notification system was 50percent inaccurate and that there was more of a problem than anybody realised, also that there was no support for people. It went from there. My telephone number was made available and I had so many calls from so many people, who had been suffering for years.

It was true that Stroud had a significantly higher incidence of meningitis than the average. As we found out later on, the disease does move in clusters and there is a higher incidence in different places. Meningitis is a bacterium which invades a community and which moves around, which is why mass antibiotics are not the answer.

So we set up the Meningitis Trust. We wanted to set up a support line, promote research and, more importantly, awareness. The Health Authority was not pleased: GPs were being inundated. The council did not like us either: people weren't coming to Stroud, they wouldn't use our swimming pools, and nobody would buy our houses. But all we wanted was to educate people, give them the signs and symptoms. There were a lot of tussles, we had some heated debates, but we knew what we were talking about and we had huge public support.

Eventually the Health Authority realised we were not troublemakers, that we were simply saying, 'This is happening in our town, come on, let's do something about it.' In 1987 a study was commissioned in Stonehouse: 98percent of the population turned out to give blood and saliva samples, which showed how much commitment people had. From that, they found out that there was a higher percentage in the area than the average, and they are still using the study now, even though it was nearly twenty years ago. It was one of the biggest studies ever undertaken in this country. We had huge support, including Professor Moxon in Oxford, who was instrumental in the HIB vaccine. The vaccine is now given to all newborn babies at two, three and four months and 98percent of cases were gone in two years.

This is what Stroud is all about: if we think we can do something, we get on and do it. The Trust came about because of a mixture of the right people at the right time. It was phenomenon, but it was a Stroud phenomenon! I used to take things as they were; I don't any more. Being part of the Meningitis Trust has changed my whole life.

I am vice-chairman of the Trust now; I was chairman in the past. The Trust is so exciting, we have achieved so much: two vaccines, first HIB and then in 1999 Meningococcal C. I am so proud of it. It was a lot of hard work and determination, a lot of sticking your head above the parapet, and in the early days it was a campaigning organisation, which it isn't so much now, because we have the support of the health authority and we advise other countries too.

Hopefully there will be a vaccine for Meningococcal B within the next five to eight years. Once it is found, we will have to change as an organisation. Our current campaign is 'Support for Life' which is about helping those who have been damaged by the disease: amputees and brain-damaged individuals. We provide help lines, support and education.

I was awarded a doctorate from the Southampton University for Services to Social Sciences in July 1988 and I was awarded the MBE on 12 June 2004 and went to Buckingham Palace to receive it on 21 October. I accepted it on behalf of all those people who helped us at the Trust and for the community as a whole, who have made Stroud really proud of its unique charity.

Jane Wells MBE

The Stroud Pound

An ideal place for this system to work

I read a book called *After the Crash: The Emergence of a Rainbow Economy* by Guy Dauncey in about 1989. We had moved to Stroud in 1972 and were living in Chalford. The book was inspirational and the ideas contained within it were community-based and very empowering. The book talked about the LETS system – Local Exchange and Trading Systems. LETS allow members to trade goods or services without conventional money using a local credit or currency. Members allow themselves to be listed in a directory with a description of what they can offer.

It occurred to me that Stroud was just the sort of place that this sort of self-help system would thrive: the town has always had a strong sense of community and is neither too big nor too small. I began talking about the possibilities with Sandra Bruce, who really helped to get the whole thing off the ground. Once it was up and running, Eric Von Nida and John Rhodes also became central to the scheme.

We discovered that the scheme was running successfully in Totnes in Devon and we went to visit the town and the LETS organisers. When we ourselves subsequently called a public meeting in Stroud, a member of the Totnes group came as a visiting speaker and talked about his group's experiences.

The basic premise is a good one and when you float the idea to people, they generally think it can work: it is basically an extended barter system, within which you exchange goods or services and receive credits in return, which are redeemable within the group. Most people charge what they would normally charge, but instead of quoting in pound sterling, they charge in 'Stroud pounds'. There is a chequebook system and cheques are added to or subtracted from a member's account.

The Stroud pound took off in a big way in the '90s and, at its height, we had about 400 people as registered members. We had a lot of publicity and it became an extremely successful organisation. Unfortunately, it lost its momentum and although it is still running, it does so these days at a much lower ebb. Westill have a chequebook system, but ideally we would now offer a credit card instead.

As far as I am concerned, however, the ideas and possibilities of the Stroud pound are as valid as they ever were. It works particularly well for self-employed people, less so for commercial services. Stroud is still an ideal place for the system to work: we have so many artists, craftspeople, and natural therapists in the town, all of whom are predisposed to such an idea. Most of these people, and indeed most traders in Stroud nowadays, are what I call 'blow-ins', but nevertheless, they are all people who have been attracted to Stroud because of it's alternative spirit and society. The Stroud Valleys have traditionally drawn these people to them, going back to the Arts and Crafts Movement and of course, the early community experiments at Whiteway. Today, Rudolf Steiner's anthroposophical movement is strongly represented in the town, particularly at the Centre for Science and Art in Lansdown.

Maggie Mills

The Stroud Preservation Trust

Conservation isn't just about saying no

In the aftermath of the High Street campaign, although we had achieved a victory in terms of saving the listed buildings, members of SHSAG were still seen to be negative in many ways and were given some bad press. A positive new direction was required and

THIS CRUMBLING FACADE HIDES
A MEDIEVAL HALL (probably Stroud's oldest building)

33 L. PET SHOP 895 33

CAN IT BE SAVED?

A vision of Stroud in around the late 1960s. Men talk outside a derelict building, now known as the Medieval Hall.

the Stroud Preservation Trust was formed. I became its first chairman.

Julian Usborne

Sold for £1

In 1965, when Gloucestershire County Council had originally planned the great ring road, they bought six buildings at the top of the High Street. The Stroud Preservation Trust realised that the lower three of the six buildings in question were medieval and came up with a scheme: that the County Council could demolish the upper three buildings, allowing them to pedestrianise the High Street and build Cornhill, but that they should then give the lower three buildings to the Trust. This is what happened. In fact, they sold them to us for £1.

Anne Mackintosh

Town centre regeneration

The Trust's project number one became known as 'the medieval hall', which is the last block of buildings on the right at the top of the High Street, where Bishopston Trading is now. We set up a community programme and we restored the buildings, which took us about eighteen months. We employed researchers and archaeologists and it turned out to be a very ancient building, 1539, one of the oldest in Stroud. It was a great success and we were able to demonstrate that conservation isn't just about saying no.

In 1984 our second project was another town centre regeneration: No. 55 High Street and Withey's Yard. This was a Georgian building whose classical façade was marred by an ugly twentieth-century shop front; we bought it for £70,000. Until then, developers had only been interested in retail property that faced the main road; they didn't want to know about the upper floors or the land at the back. We wanted to show that you could take

a derelict building and use all the surrounding land, which we did. We rebuilt and redeveloped the building and its rear courtyard, providing high quality commercial and residential units. Twenty years on, the café and shops are still flourishing.

The Trust had made some money on these last projects and, despite a property slump in the late '80s, we could afford to look for projects which were worth doing, even if they weren't going to make money. I left at that point, but I was there long enough to buy the Goods Shed at Stroud station. We had grand ideas about turning it into a cinema or theatre.

Julian Usborne

A hands-on organisation

What brought the Goods Shed to our attention in the first place was the grandness of the building, neither listed nor protected in any way, which British Rail wanted to demolish. We bought it on a long lease, immediately got it Grade II listed and began fundraising in order to put its roof back on. Funding came from English Heritage, the District Council and also from the Trust itself.

We started looking for a user to take the building from us: there were several commercial and charitable options open to us, but for various reasons, none came to fruition. The building is still standing though, it is now listed Grade II and it is safeguarded, awaiting its future.

In 1987, another project came into view. The Toll House at Cainscross (past Tricorn House on the left-hand side) and the two houses behind it were in very poor condition and in desperate need of repair. The owners, the Co-op, were eventually persuaded, after pressure from the council, to sell the buildings to us and we made them into three separate houses. In 1990 we bought Arundel Mill

William Waldegrave, Environment Minister, hands over the Goods Shed keys to Julian Usborne (even though there were no doors on the building at all!), 1986.

House and cottages, off the London Road. Again, the house was ruinous and dangerous: we sold some of its land to fund repairs and with further grant funding, created seven houses on the site.

Stroud Preservation Trust has always been a hands-on organisation with a loyal band of supporters. Set up as a charitable company, we are one of over 250 revolving fund building preservation trusts in the UK, many of which featured on the recent television series *Restoration*. We work closely with architects, structural engineers and contractors, paying for their services.

It is important to recognise that times have changed a lot since we first established the Trust. There is not nearly so much dereliction in Stroud and, happily, our projects have acted as a catalyst for change in each area: the High Street, for example, has been pedestrianised and almost every property has been repaired or renovated. In Cainscross too, change of ownership brought subsequent improvement to the row of shops beyond the Toll House. We attempted, unsuccessfully, to buy No. 15 High Street, the old Smith and Lee building, which is one of the few town centre buildings in severe disrepair. It is in great need of our intervention, if only we could acquire it. Since then, of course, we have repaired the Arch at Paganhill as our Millennium Project.

Anne Mackintosh

Other local titles published by Tempus

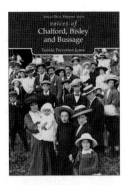

Voices of Chalford, Bisley and Bussage
TAMSIN TREVERTON JONES

This book brings together the personal memories of people who have lived and grown up in the Chalford, Chalford Hill, France Lynch, Eastcombe, Bussage, Brownshill and Bisley during the last century. Reminiscences range from childhood games, shops and transport to the war years and local characters. The stories are complemented by over 100 photographs drawn from the private collections of the contributors.

0 7524 3204 4

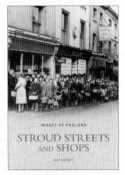

Stroud Streets and Shops
WILF MERRETT

With over 150 photographs, postcards and advertisements, *Stroud Streets and Shops* captures the town's commercial heritage and offers a glimpse into the past. At the beginning of the twentieth century, there were a diversity of shops in Stroud offering everything the casual shopper or housewife needed. The town has seen many changes since then and this book recalls Stroud in the days before the arrival of supermarkets and shopping malls.

0 7524 3307 5

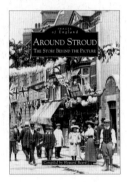

Around Stroud
The Story Behind The Picture
HOWARD BEARD

Around Stroud recalls some of the events and personalities which shaped the Stroud area in the early twentieth century. Amongst the 100 old pictures and other archive ephemera which illustrate this volume are snapshots of the arrival of the first railcars and motor buses as well as photographs of Coronation celebrations, May Day revels and Empire Day festivities.

0 7524 1577 8

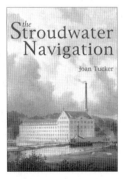

The Stroudwater Navigation
JOAN TUCKER

The Stroudwater Navigation opened in 1779 from the Severn at Framilode to Stroud, a distance of eight miles. It brought increased prosperity to the Stroud valleys, a centre for early industrialisation. Ten years later the Thames & Severn Canal linked with it. The Stroudwater is unique for being in the hands of the original company for over 200 years, and most of the primary material for this book, including illustrations, paintings, photographs and plans, derives from the company archive.

0 7524 2806 3

If you are interested in purchasing other books published by Tempus, or in case you have difficulty finding any Tempus books in your local bookshop, you can also place orders directly through our website

www.tempus-publishing.com